AUTHOR

Linda Fallon was born in Cork, and alt
travel bug early in life and had left town I
feels entitled to wear her ethically-trade
Republic of Cork T-shirt with pride whe
studied at University College Cork (UC
on and off since then.

C000194154

FEEDBACK REQUEST

Pubs, restaurants, tourist attractions – they open up and shut down with alarming
rapidity, quality can vary as businesses change hands, some places go downhill and
others become the next big thing. If you have any comments about your trip to
Cork feel free to drop me a line at fallonlinda@yahoo.co.uk or write to me c/o
Bradt Travel Guides, 23 High Street, Chalfont St Peter, Bucks SL9 9QE.

AUTHOR STORY

Cork is a quirky place to visit and a quirky place to write about. My favourite query, and the query I get most often from the copy-editors and proofreaders at Bradt is always, 'you haven't included a phone number for XXX, does this place really not have a phone?' Inevitably, the place really doesn't. And what of it? It's nice to be able to step off a busy high street - awash with the same chains you find everywhere else – into a pub that hasn't made any nod to the 20th century, never mind the 21st. That's typical Cork: forward-looking, but at its own pace. Sometimes the place drives me mad, the rain, the puddles – trying to take research notes with an inside-out umbrella in one hand, a sodden notebook in the other and water soaking through your shoes is really over-rated as a cultural experience. At the very least I didn't have to put any gloss on that, the great thing about writing for Bradt guides is that you can write about the place exactly as you find it. So yes, I might give out about the rain (maybe even exaggerate a little for effect), but still, wild horses wouldn't separate me from my ethically-traded organic cotton People's Republic of Cork t-shirt. It's changed a lot since I first moved there and I expect it will continue to change quite dramatically over the next few years, and while I go back there for what I know and love about the place, it's always exciting to see what it's got to offer next.

St Finbarre's Cathedral at night (CK) page 177

Port of Cork city (AT/RH)

Cork

the Bradt City Guide

Linda Fallon

www.bradtguides.com

Bradt Travel Guides Ltd, UK
The Globe Pequot Press Inc, USA

edition
2

Blarney Castle (JL/RH) page 193

KISSING THE BLARNEY STONE

Acknowledgements

I have so many people to thank for their help with this book that I can't possibly fit them all in. There are a few, however, who deserve special mention: enormous thanks to James Boyd for thinking of me in the first place, and for his tremendous support; Emma Thomson at Bradt for all her hard work, Brendan Duffy for his all-weather intrepidity, good humour and resourcefulness; Laura McGloughlin for much thoughtfulness; Pat Cotter, Seamus O'Tuama, Ali Robertson and John Miller for their help; Dondo for the use of his computer; and Clara for all her suggestions. Special thanks to Paul for all his help, and of course, to my family and friends.

Contents

Introduction   VII

How to Use this Book   x

1   **Contexts**   1
History 2, Economy 9, People 9, Cultural etiquette 9, Giving
something back/Local charities 10, Business 10, Religion 10, Culture
and festivals 11, Sport 18, Geography and climate 23

2   **Planning**   25
The city – a practical overview 25, When to visit 28, Suggested
itineraries 39, Tourist offices 40, Tour operators 41, Red tape 43,
Getting there and away 45, Time 48, Health and safety 49, What to
take 49, Money and budgeting 50

3   **Practicalities**   53
Banks and money matters 53, Communications 55, Media 57,
Embassies and consulates 58, Medical services 59, Religious
services 60, Local tour operators 60, Other practicalities 63

4   **Local Transport**   **64**
Buses 64, Trains 66, Taxis and cabs 66, Airport transfer 67, Car hire 68,
Parking 69, Bike hire 70

5   **Accommodation**   **71**
Hotels 72, Guesthouses 80, Hostels 82, Self-catering 84

6   **Eating and Drinking**   **86**
Restaurants 87, Cafés 108, Bars and pubs serving food 114, Takeaways 115, Further afield 117, Drinking 119

7   **Entertainment and Nightlife**   **131**
Nightclubs 131, Gay/Lesbian 132, Theatre and opera 134, Cinema 135,
Live music venues 137

8   **Shopping**   **139**
Antiques 140, Alternative 140, Bookshops 142, Clothes and
fashion 143, Food and wine 145, Gifts 147, Home furnishings 148,
Jewellery 148, Music 148, Outdoor shops 149,
Supermarkets/department stores/shopping centres 150

9   **Walking Tours**   **153**
Walk 1 – city centre 153, Walk 2 – circling the city centre 158

10 Sightseeing   **167**
Art galleries 167, Museums 171, Churches/cathedrals 176, Other
attractions 178, Parks and lakes 187, Entertaining the children 189

11 Beyond the City   **192**
Heritage cards 192, Blarney 193, Cobh 195, Fota 199, Gougane Barra
Forest Park 201, Kinsale 202, Midleton 208

12 Language   **213**
Irish 214, Cork slang 220

13 Further Information   **221**
Entertainment 221, Maps 221, Books 221, Gay Cork 222,
Websites 222

Index   **224**

Introduction

'The real capital', as it is fondly known by all its proud inhabitants, embraced its 2005 European Capital of Culture status eagerly. Cork is no stranger to culture, with a rich literary, musical and sporting heritage –which it drew upon throughout the year. More laid-back than Dublin, it is an easygoing, friendly city, compact and easy to get around. Popular with foodies and music-lovers alike, from the Old English Market to the Guinness Jazz Festival, there's something for everyone here.

When I first moved to Cork as a student I got buses everywhere, got lost in the maze of side streets, confused one bridge with another and spent a lot of time in the many discreetly located pubs – no dark lane was left unturned. In no time at all I had oriented myself, had put the bus money towards an umbrella and had finally got a handle on the plethora of pubs available.

The Capital of Culture designation was just the incentive Cork needed to give itself a decent makeover. Money has been poured into revamping the overall look of the city and the improvement has been both aesthetic and practical (yet another bridge has been added; you can never have too many bridges if you're a city based on an island). The city has a much more modern European feel to it now but still retains its Irish stamp, broad leafy boulevards and sidewalk cafés (the latter given a boost by the indoors smoking ban) lying shoulder-to-shoulder with old men's pubs and the odd renegade pothole.

An engaging city in its own right, the 2005 programme made Cork an even more attractive and interesting destination. The year kicked off with some shocking weather, lashing rain, stereotypically Irish; it didn't bode well for the opening ceremony and accompanying intricate fireworks display scheduled for the first week of January. However, on the day in question, by some minor miracle, it stopped raining. I didn't have a quay-side ticket, but I had a pretty good spot outside Merchant's Quay Shopping Centre and managed to see a lot of the fireworks over Patrick's Bridge as well as others reflected in the various windows around me. This was the start of the year that saw such imaginative projects as IRIS – a canny exploration of the city's inhabitants in action. Ten thousand rings were distributed throughout the city, and whenever two wearers met each other they had have an agreed physical or mental reaction. Reactions varied widely; agreeing to go for a swift pint was not unheard of. Thus this piece of 'art' had a life of its own, and probably still does to this day. Over a million people attended the official 2005 events. The events themselves came about from a public call for ideas and the resulting programme comprised local, national and international suggestions; it was very much an inclusive, Euro-culture year. Other highlights included a John Berger exhibition at the Vangard Gallery and a series of readings by authors such as Seamus Heaney and Doris Lessing; the first Frank O'Connor International Short Story Award was given to Yiyun Li for her collection A Thousand Years of Good Prayers; Daniel Libeskind's Eighteen Turns, an architectural pavilion, was on display at Fota House; art, literature, language, music, photography, food, dance, drama, multi-media, film, sport, Irish culture – it was all celebrated. Indeed Cork continues to celebrate these things; just because it no longer holds the title does not mean that it will cease to be a capital of culture.

The broadly curving Patrick Street is undoubtedly Cork's 'main' street and a good platform for helping you to get your bearings, but Cork is so compact that every other little alleyway is equally important in terms of nightlife, eating out and shopping. This is what makes the city centre so interesting to explore. The narrow side streets aren't just routes from one useful main street to another; they are all treasures in themselves. Streets and alleys aside, you are never too far away from the countryside either. You don't have to drive through miles of urban sprawl to find a bit of green – it's just a few minutes away. Even within the city, the streets are tree-lined (come in April for the fleeting beauty of the cherry blossoms; come in autumn for the crisp leaf-filled air), there are parks, there's the river – there's never any fear of urban claustrophobia setting in.

Cork has a warmth that is harder to detect in a bigger city like Dublin. It's personable and charming. The people are friendly and approachable and have wonderfully lilting accents. There's always lots going on, but if you don't feel like 'lots', it's also the perfect place to kick back and recharge your batteries. It's a city where you'll feel instantly at ease and that I think you will always earmark for a return visit.

How to Use this Book

H Dúchas sites (see page 192).

MAP REFERENCES (eg: [B2]) These relate to the colour map section at the end of the book.

EMAIL ADDRESSES/WEBSITES These are given wherever possible.

RESTAURANT PRICES These do not include service charges although some places have a 10% service charge for parties over a certain number. I have indicated this where relevant. Tipping is usually around 10%.

ACCOMMODATION Room rates are per room per night, bed and breakfast rates include breakfast and are per person sharing per night. Hotels are divided between airport, city centre, south of the city centre and east of the city centre. Within those categories, the most expensive or luxurious is first, followed by the others in descending order.

PRICES Those quoted in the text were correct at the time of going to press but it can be reasonably expected that they will have gone up in the meantime.

OPENING HOURS Last orders in most restaurants are usually around 22.00. Some close between lunch and dinner, usually from about 15.00 to 18.00, but others stay open all day. Many are closed on Sundays. Pubs are open Monday to Thursday 10.30–23.30 (plus 30 minutes drinking-up time), Friday and Saturday 10.30–00.30 (plus 30 minutes), Sunday noon to 23.00 (plus 30 minutes). Pubs with bar extensions open till 01.30 (plus 30 minutes). All pubs are closed Christmas Day and Good Friday. Christmas Eve and Holy Thursday have midweek opening hours. If a Sunday is followed by a Bank Holiday it will have Saturday opening hours.

CREDIT CARDS Most places will accept payment by Visa or MasterCard. American Express and Diners are less widely accepted.

DEBIT CARDS Irish debit cards only are accepted.

CORK AT A GLANCE

Location Southern coast of Ireland, 254km from Dublin, 208km from Rosslare Harbour, 128km from Shannon Airport

Climate Average temperatures: winter 7°C, spring and autumn 13°C, summer 18°C. There can be up to 18 hours of daylight during the summer but there's always the possibility of rain. Approx 1,000mm of rain per annum

Population 123,338 in the city; 448,181 in the county (2002)

Currency Euro exchange rate € 1 / £0.68 sterling / US$1.31 (March 2007)

Time Winter GMT; summer GMT + 1 hour

International telephone code +353

Local telephone code 021

Public holidays 1 January, 17 March (St Patrick's Day), Good Friday, Easter Monday, May Day (first Monday in May), June holiday (first Monday in June), August holiday (first Monday in August), October holiday (last Monday in October), 25–26 December

1 Contexts

'The Rebel County', 'the Real Capital' – with such epithets Cork emphasises its status as Ireland's second city and as the 2005 European Capital of Culture. An attractive town that welcomes all, Cork is ideal for pedestrians. Its unique character comes across in the calls of the Echo Boys and the sounds of the Shandon Bells pealing across the banks of the Lee.

With a rich cultural, sporting and culinary heritage, the effervescence of Cork and its proud citizens is immediately apparent to all who visit. This is the kind of city that you will always come back to – one visit is never enough – especially as it has such a range of world-renowned festivals scattered throughout the year. Some people think of the city as simply a gateway to west Cork; it is, of course, an ideal starting point for a trip along the west coast, but it's a fun destination in its own right.

This guide hopes to give you some idea of how much such a small city has to offer. From Café Paradiso (reputedly the best vegetarian restaurant in Ireland) and the annual film festival to the Gaelic Games and Fota Wildlife Park, the city is full of gaiety and good living and quite simply, it's an easy destination. There's nothing complicated about Cork; it's a great place to unwind and enjoy the simpler and finer things in life. Take things at your own pace; nobody is going to rush you. Surely this is what holidays are all about?

HISTORY

Cork city has its beginnings in the 7th century when it was founded as a monastic settlement by a monk named Finbarre, supposedly on the site of today's St Finbarre's Cathedral. Indeed, St Finbarre is now the patron saint of Cork. The name Cork comes from *Corcaigh*, which is Irish for 'marshy', since Cork was originally a series of 13 marshy islands, the drainage and reclamation of which took place during the Georgian and Victorian eras. The main streets were once river channels, the evidence of which can still be seen today in the bollards and road-level arches where the boats used to moor.

To our knowledge, Cork was first attacked by the Norwegian Vikings in AD820 and many of the Hermitage's valuables were taken. Several more attacks ensued over the next 100 years leading to the building of defensive towers, one of which survived until the 18th century when it started to deteriorate to the point where there was nothing left.

The Norse settled in Cork, developing a sort of Viking town thought to have been located around the present-day South Main Street. There they coexisted in relative peace with the neighbouring Celtic clans, even inter-marrying, although they continued to keep their settlements coastal by nature, to facilitate swift escapes should the need arise.

Around AD914 the Danish Vikings invaded, taking over the existing Norwegian settlements and staying there. They also built their own larger settlements, one of which would have been on an island, now the site of the Beamish and Crawford Brewery.

In 1169 the Anglo-Normans, led by Strongbow, arrived in Ireland and disrupted the power-sharing agreement between the Vikings and one of the most important Irish clans at the time, the McCarthys. The Normans attacked Cork and after a fierce battle they finally defeated the Danes and the Irish. They commemorated the victory with a church dedicated to St Nicholas, whom the Normans revered. There is still a St Nicholas Church on the same site off Douglas Street, although it is not the original. Other changes effected by the Normans included shortening the city name from Corcach Mór na Mumhan to the more manageable Corke. This was significant in that it was the first anglicisation of the Irish language.

Then, in 1185, Cork's first royal charter was granted by Prince John. This entitled the city to numerous privileges, including the protection of the Crown.

By the late 13th century the city was enclosed by high walls. The two entry points were at the North Gate and South Gate bridges. In 1300 the population was estimated at 800 and the Corporation of Cork, a municipal, legal and administrative body, was formed by the wealthier merchants. The walled town developed further as a port and market town during the 14th century.

In the mid 16th century the Augustinian, Dominican and Franciscan abbeys were closed by Henry VIII. The Crown asserted its dominance, constructing Elizabeth

Fort in 1601 after local clans had laid siege to the city. This was the year in which the English defeated the Irish–Spanish alliance at the Battle of Kinsale.

In 1649 Cork Corporation, fearful of a massacre similar to that in Drogheda, surrendered to Cromwell before the arrival of his army. For the next 30 years Catholic citizens were under severe restrictions. The city's first bank was established in 1680. In 1688, the Catholic King James II arrived in Cork to incite a rebellion against the Protestant Pretender, William of Orange. In September 1690 the Jacobite army took control of the city and in the resulting siege William of Orange's forces, led by the Duke of Marlborough, levelled most of the old city walls (remnants of which may be seen in Bishop Lucey Park). A cannon used during the siege is embedded in the footpath beside the park on the corner of Tuckey Street and the Grand Parade and a cannonball fired at St Finbarre's Cathedral may be found in the ambulatory.

Over the next few years the old city walls were dismantled and the city was rebuilt amidst the reclamation of the marshes. The Quaker community had been in Cork since 1655 but it was only in the early 18th century that they were allowed to develop their own land (around Grattan Street and Fenn's Quay). Huguenots, who had fled religious persecution in France, developed Lavitt's Quay, Academy Street, French Church Street and Carey's Lane. The North Gate and South Gate bridges were replaced by bridges of cut stone. In 1719 the Cornmarket was constructed and Edward Webber, the town clerk, built a walk called the Meer-Dyke on which he erected Cork's first tea house.

The town's custom house was relocated to Emmet Place in 1720 and the Royal Cork Yacht Club was founded. In the 1720s several churches were built, including St Ann's, Christ Church, St Nicholas and St Peter's.

In 1776 Nano Nagle founded the Presentation Sisters in Douglas Street, providing food, medicine and a basic education for the poor.

The population more than doubled at this time and the town boasted 30 breweries and ten distilleries. Watchmen were employed to patrol the city to protect the citizenry and an 11 o'clock curfew was enforced.

In 1787 the 'lord mayor' received the gold chain that is still used. In 1788 the English Market was established providing fresh produce similar to what may be found there today.

Cork Harbour Commissioners was established in 1813 and a new custom house was built in 1814. Washington Street was opened in 1824 after the clearance of a large slum around South Main Street. Gas street lights were used from June 1825 and in 1831 Western Road was completed.

From the 1830s new and elaborate municipal buildings such as the Courthouse, the City Gaol and the County Gaol were erected and several Catholic churches were built as a result of the Catholic Emancipation Act of 1829. It was around this time that Father Theobald Mathew founded a temperance movement.

In 1838, the *Sirius*, the first passenger steamship to cross the Atlantic, left Cork.

By 1840 many citizens were facing starvation and there was only one institution for caring for the impoverished, the House of Industry in Blackpool. The city had suffered a recession after the Napoleonic Wars and in spite of the municipal development the population had fallen. In 1845, the Great Potato Famine meant that the situation in the city worsened. A variety of relief schemes were organised resulting in the repair of the marina, the construction of Carrigrohane Straight Road, the path around the lough and the building of the university.

Queen Victoria visited Cork in 1849 and in this year a railway to Dublin was introduced. In the 1850s and 1860s new and decorative buildings were erected. In 1864 the statue of Father Mathew was unveiled on Patrick Street, in 1865 the foundation was laid for St Finbarre's Cathedral and in 1869 the foundation was laid for the North Cathedral. Queen Victoria visited Cork again in 1900 and the title for the first citizen was changed to Lord Mayor.

The adulation of the queen's first visit (when Cobh changed its name to Queenstown) was no longer apparent. Brian Dillon and Jeremiah O'Donovan Rossa and the Irish Republican Brotherhood had gained much public support. The Campaign for Home Rule was becoming more popular and indeed it was a Corkman, Michael Collins, that helped lead Ireland to independence.

In 1902, Lord Mayor Edward Fitzgerald organised an international exhibition to show what the city had to offer. When the exhibition ended and all the pavilions were taken down a public park was laid out on the site and named after the lord mayor.

During World War I, in 1917, Henry Ford's first European factory was built in Cork. At that time many Corkmen were fighting in the army.

TRACING YOUR IRISH ANCESTORS

There are millions of people the world over who can claim to be of Irish descent. Somewhere in the region of six million people emigrated from Ireland over the years following the Great Famine in the 19th century. Understandably many of those descendants are keen to know more about their ancestors and the country they hailed from. This, however, is easier said than done, as there isn't any one centre in Ireland dedicated purely to every aspect of genealogy. The best thing to do is to get in touch with the Genealogical Office in the National Library (*www.nli.ie*) in Dublin. Once in Cork, advice on genealogical research is available from the Local History librarian on the top floor of Cork City Library on Grand Parade. Alternatively the Cobh Heritage Centre (see page 198) offers a genealogy record-finder service for approximately €25. To avail of this service, you must know the name of the town or village from which your ancestors came. You can access the service online at www.cobhheritage.com. Knowing your ancestor's full name and religion as well as important dates (birth, marriage, death) will help you track down the relevant records. The website www.irishorigins.com is also useful.

In March 1920, Lord Mayor Tomas MacCurtain was found murdered in his home. It was suggested that he was killed by the Royal Irish Constabulary on behalf of the British government. In October of the same year Lord Mayor Terence MacSwiney died after a 74-day hunger strike in Brixton Prison. In November Tom Barry's Flying Column killed 20 British soldiers in an ambush near Kilmichael. In December IRA men ambushed British auxiliaries within a few hundred metres of the main barracks, and in retaliation the Black and Tans set fire to much of the city. The eastern side of Patrick Street, City Hall and the Carnegie Library all suffered. The British Government aided the building of a new City Hall in 1932.

City buses were brought to Cork in 1931 and the tram services that had operated since 1898 came to an end. Gas was replaced by electricity for street lighting in 1936. In 1949 the telephone exchange was made automatic and in 1954 the first automated traffic lights were introduced.

In 1955 the Opera House was gutted by fire and in 1961 Cork Airport was opened. In 1963 President Kennedy was made a Freeman of the City during his visit in June. In 1965 the new Cork Opera House was opened.

In 1966 Jack Lynch, who had won All-Ireland medals for both hurling and Gaelic football for Cork, became Taoiseach (Irish Prime Minister) and negotiated Ireland's entry to the EU (then the EEC). In 1998 the Jack Lynch Tunnel, named in his honour, was opened.

The Opera House has experienced a facelift in recent times and Patrick Street and its offshoots have been redesigned by Barcelona architect Beth Galí; the same look is being extended to Grand Parade. In 2005 Cork was European Capital of Culture, a mantle the city carried off with aplomb. In 2006 the new state-of-the-art terminal was opened at Cork Airport.

ECONOMY

Since the Celtic Tiger boom of the 1990s, many Irish people have certainly enjoyed a more affluent lifestyle. Unemployment rates dropped, people had more money to spend. Things have levelled off now and new problems have arisen. While it's no problem for many to indulge in weekend city breaks on the Continent, property is now the greener grass, with fewer people than ever able to afford their own home. Property prices continue to spiral out of control and more and more people are unwilling to commit to the massive mortgages involved. Ireland has never been a cheap place to live, and 'Rip-off Ireland' is a term being bandied about increasingly by all and sundry. Nevertheless, most people enjoy a comfortable lifestyle.

PEOPLE

Corkonians are renowned for being friendly and sociable. There's such an influx of visitors every year for all the various festivals that they have to be!

CULTURAL ETIQUETTE

Never refer to Britain as 'the mainland'. Other than that, Irish people are pretty easygoing and informal – it would be hard to cause offence.

GIVING SOMETHING BACK/LOCAL CHARITIES

The **Cork Simon Community** *(PO Box 76, Togher, Cork;* ✆ *021 432 1166;* **e** *info@ signupforsimon.com; www.simoncommunity.com)* has been caring and campaigning for homeless people in Cork since 1971. They have an emergency shelter on Anderson's Quay, and a few residential houses. They operate a nightly soup run, providing hot meals, blankets, advice and companionship for dozens of people every week. They rely heavily on public support and volunteer work and donations are always appreciated. They have a Simon shop on North Main Street and welcome donations of good quality clothing and other items.

BUSINESS

Business hours in the city are generally Monday to Friday, 09.00–17.30.

RELIGION

Roughly 90% of the Irish population is Roman Catholic, an unsurprising fact in a country often referred to as 'the island of saints and scholars'. The Catholic Church has always had the country in a vice-like grip, but its influence has weakened considerably over the last decade or so and church attendance is dropping all the time with an increasing number of people falling into the lapsed-Catholic category. Nevertheless churches are still relatively full on Sundays, church weddings are as popular as ever and pilgrimages to places such as Lourdes and Medjugorje are still on the go. Irish laws still reflect conservative Catholic views, divorce has been available in the country only since 1995 and abortions are still illegal although it is not illegal to provide information on them.

CULTURE AND FESTIVALS

The Irish are a party people, Corkonians included. There is almost always something going on and Cork's 2005 status as European Capital of Culture guaranteed that festivities would always be top of the agenda. Many of the events organised for 2005 have found a lasting home in Cork's cultural future. (See *When to visit* in *Chapter 2*, pages 28–39, for annual festivals.) Random events aside, Cork has a rich literary, musical and artistic heritage which is still alive and kicking today as is evidenced by the wealth of art galleries, singer-songwriter nights and literary festivals.

ART There are several art galleries in Cork (see *Sightseeing* chapter, pages 167–71, for a full list of galleries) and plenty of people and projects to watch out for. The Crawford Municipal Art Gallery and the Fenton Gallery should not be missed. Local artists include Maud Cotter, Tom Climent, Vivian Roche and Billy Foley. If you are going to Cobh it's worth visiting the Sirius Arts Centre. The Cork Artists Collective, which comprises graduates of the Crawford Art College, is a group of artists actively involved in arts culture. Located in an 18th-century building in the grounds of St Finbarre's Cathedral, the collective holds an annual exhibition within the cathedral itself. Art Trail,

11

LITERARY CORK

In August 1856 **Charles Dickens** was scheduled to give a reading in the Athenaeum (now the Opera House) in the city centre. On his way into the city he passed Monsfield House on the Rochestown road near Douglas. Legend has it that the house was the tragic scene of a fatal wedding breakfast. The wedding ceremony had just ended and the newly married bride returned to her father's house for the reception. There she encountered her former lover whose erstwhile poverty had caused her to end the relationship. He had since made his fortune and had now returned to ask for her hand in marriage, only to find her just married to another. The bride killed herself in despair and fell dead across the dining table. Her corpse was removed but the dining room was left intact for a generation. *Great Expectations* and the unfortunate Miss Havisham came out five years later in 1861. Monsfield House is no longer there but the nearby Havisham House keeps the story alive.

Wild West as it sounds, **Edmund Spenser** was actually Sheriff of Cork for a while.

an artist-led and artist-oriented group, provides an annual opportunity for the public to experience the work of contemporary artists in Cork (see *Chapter 2*, pages 37–8).

LITERATURE With a variety of annual literature festivals (see *When to visit* in *Chapter 2*, pages 28–39), there's no question Cork has a thriving bookish scene. Poets, novelists, short-story writers, playwrights – the city has no shortage of wordsmiths

He lived off North Main Street and was married in Christ Church on South Main Street in 1594. He spent 20 years living in Ireland, and Doneraile in North Cork provided the backdrop for his most famous work, *The Faerie Queene*.

James Joyce visited Cork as a child when his father, who was from Sunday's Well, was selling off some of the family property. Joyce drew on this experience when he described Stephen Dedalus's trip to Cork in *A Portrait of the Artist as a Young Man*. Stephen and his father, Simon, stay in the Victoria Hotel on Patrick Street and even order *drisheen* (see box, *Chapter 6*, pages 98–9) for breakfast.

Having spent some time living in Mallow, **Anthony Trollope** went on to write *Castle Richmond*, a novel of the Great Famine.

Herman Melville never made it to Cork, but the film *Moby Dick*, directed by John Huston, although set in New England, was actually filmed in Youghal in east Cork.

who may or may not take their inspiration from their post-prandial perambulations along the banks of the Lee. From the short-story genius of Frank O'Connor (see box, *Chapter 10*, pages 182–3) to the pithy poems of Gerry Murphy, you can pretty much pick your genre and there will almost certainly be a Cork writer of note that you can refer to. Other names to look out for are Seán O'Faoláin (see pages 14–15), Seán Ó Riordáin, Conal Creedon, Enda Walsh, Pat Cotter, Liz O'Donoghue, Greg Delanty,

SEÁN O'FAOLÁIN

Born John Whelan on 22 February 1900 at 16 Half Moon Street opposite the stage door of the Cork Opera House, Seán O'Faoláin, who always used the Irish version of his name in his writing, had a strict upbringing by his RIC (Royal Irish Constabulary) constable father and his very pious mother. It wasn't all prayers and dreariness, however, as they also took in lodgers to earn a bit of extra money, and more often than not these were actors in town to perform in the Opera House. The family home had a high turnover of performers who seemed to John and his brothers to be almost as exotic as the characters they played. This early exposure to theatre developed into a fine appreciation as John's tastes eventually outgrew the crowd-pleasing comedies and melodramas, turning their attention instead to greater works of art and literature, such as those of Monet, Ibsen, Yeats and Hardy.

With this artistic growth came a development of John's social and political beliefs. Family holidays at his aunt's home in Rathkeale, Co Limerick, fostered an appreciation for all things rural. A city boy, he began to see the Irish landscape with new eyes and to feel the first rumblings of his nascent Republican leanings, later fighting on the Republican side in the Civil War.

Gregory O'Donoghue, Trevor Joyce, William Trevor, William Wall, Tom McCarthy, Daniel Corkery and Gaye Shortland. For more information on Cork writers visit the Munster Literature Centre (see *Chapter 10*, pages 181–4).

The war left him disillusioned, however. He felt the ideals of freedom and brotherhood had been compromised and, on a more personal level, that he had betrayed his parents. By becoming an Irish volunteer he was betraying his father who was devoted to all things British and, with the Bishop of Cork's denunciation of Republicanism, he had let down his mother. He had been a bomb-maker and propagandist and had moved to Dublin to become Director of Publicity for the entire Republican movement, only returning to Cork once the war had ended.

In 1926 he moved to Boston and took up a post at Harvard, but in 1933 decided to return to Ireland where, despite his misgivings, he still felt he belonged. Having developed a love–hate relationship with Cork, however, he chose to live in Dublin, preferring to deal with his native city in a fictional capacity only.

He died in 1991 having written his autobiography, three novels and numerous collections of short stories. He is also well remembered for his work on the literary and social magazine *The Bell*.

MUSIC Cork has a well-established live music scene with a good track record in churning out talented songsters and musicians. Seán Ó Riada and his band Ceoltóirí Chualann got the ball rolling back in the 1960s when they redefined attitudes by

15

Born on 2 March 1948 in the aptly named Rock Hospital in Co Donegal, Rory Gallagher moved to Cork at the age of eight, around about the same time that he first started playing the guitar. His mother was from Cork originally and they lived above his grandparents' pub on MacCurtain Street (see page 166). When he was 15 he bought a Fender Stratocaster, one of the first of its kind in the country. He would play it for the next 32 years.

That same year, 1963, he joined the Fontana Showband, although in true rock-rebel-in-the-making style, he refused to wear the uniform. He eventually left the band and set up his own group, The Impact. Influenced by the likes of The Who, The Rolling Stones and The Kinks, they were really a rock band masquerading as a showband.

The Impact toured around Ireland, England and Germany but they eventually disbanded, after which Rory formed Taste. They became quite successful and received five encores at the Isle of Wight Festival in 1970, the musical press of the time describing them as the highlight of the event which had also featured such greats as The Doors, The Who, Leonard Cohen, Jimi Hendrix and Miles Davis.

The band split up shortly after this and Rory went solo, releasing his first album in 1971

performing traditional music to listen to for its own sake as opposed to music that was merely a background rhythm for dancers. Today we have John Spillane (the only man to perform on the American release of the otherwise all-female album after which he recorded a further 13 solo albums, attaining sales of 15 million. He toured worldwide including the US several times and recorded with Jerry Lee Lewis, Howlin' Wolf and Muddy Waters. The Rolling Stones asked him to join their band but he turned them down. Other famous admirers included Slash from Guns 'n' Roses, Johnny Marr from The Smiths, U2's Bono and The Edge, Bob Dylan, John Lennon and Jimmy Page.

He suffered from depression and tackled a fear of flying with tranquillisers, using brandy to lift him out of the depression worsened by the tranquillisers. After 10–15 years of this his liver was damaged considerably. Given paracetamol for undiagnosed abdominal pains, he finally needed a liver transplant. He went in for the operation but died of an infection in London on 14 June 1995.

Revered by rock fans the world over, Rory Gallagher has a street named after him in Paris, a corner in Temple Bar in Dublin, and a square, Rory Gallagher Place, on Paul Street in Cork. There is a statue in Rory Gallagher Place by his childhood friend Geraldine Creedon, depicting his trademark Fender Stratocaster with lyrics from the songs 'Easy Come, Easy Go' and 'Jinxed' flowing from it. Much of his material is still being released to critical acclaim.

A Woman's Heart), a very popular singer-songwriter whose songs are full of local Cork references and whose gigs invariably sell out – do try and see him if you get any chance; as well as Simple Kid, Jodavino, The Frank and Walters, Sultans of Ping,

Annette Buckley, Boa Morte, Eoin Coughlan, and Fred, to name but a few. The late blues guitarist-singer Rory Gallagher (see box on pages 16–17) grew up in Cork. There are lots of live music venues around the city centre. Some pubs specialise in traditional music, others have a more diverse range. I strongly recommend trying to catch some live music while in town – it's always a good night out.

SPORT

The Irish are a sporting nation with Gaelic football and hurling the two most popular indigenous games. Páirc Uí Chaoimh is Cork's main Gaelic Athletic Association (GAA) venue. With several golf courses within easy reach of the city, this less frenetic sport provides a popular way to unwind. The lesser-known road bowling is still very much alive in rural areas and is worth keeping an eye out for if you are driving around the county.

ATHLETICS Formed in 1884 with a view to conserving and promoting Irish culture, the GAA (Gaelic Athletic Association; ❧ 021 496 3311; www.gaa.ie) was responsible for the formalising of Gaelic football and hurling, compiling the rules that we are familiar with today. Both games are played competitively at county level all over the country, the ultimate aim being to get into the All-Ireland Finals each September in Croke Park in Dublin. Also watch out for fixtures which are listed in the *Evening Echo* and the *Irish Examiner*. If the Cork team are playing at home they play in Páirc Uí

Chaoimh. There is always an opportunity at these games to pick up your indispensable People's Republic of Cork T-shirt.

GAELIC FOOTBALL Like a hands-on cross between soccer and rugby, Gaelic football has a huge following. There are 15 players to a team and the ball can be passed in any direction by either kicking it or punching it, it can also be carried for a maximum of four steps. The goalposts are like rugby posts and the scoring is similar. A ball in the net is a goal, over the bar is a point. Three points are the equivalent of one goal.

GOLF Ireland has always been a popular destination with golfing enthusiasts and Cork is no exception. Some golf clubs offer discounts for group bookings. Enquire about these when making your reservation. Fees listed are per person.

Cork Golf Club Little Island; ✆ 021 435 3451; e corkgolfclub@eircom.net; www.corkgolfclub.ie. 18 holes. 72 par. Length of course: 6,119m (6,731 yards). Visitors welcome every day depending on availability. Club professional Peter Hickey provides tuition: €85 (midweek), €95 (weekend).
Douglas Golf Club Douglas; ✆ 021 489 5297; e admin@douglasgolfclub.ie; www.douglasgolfclub.ie. 18 holes. 72 par. Visitors welcome (excluding Tue).
East Cork Golf Club Gortacrue, Midleton; ✆ 021 463 1687; e eastcorkgolfclub@eircom.net; www.eastcorkgolfclub.com. 18 holes. 69 par. Visitors welcome. €30 all week.
Fernhill Golf & Country Club Carrigaline; ✆ 021 437 2226; e fernhill@iol.ie; www.fernhillgolfhotel.com. 18 holes. 69 par. Visitors welcome.

19

Fota Island Golf Club Carrigtwohill; ☎ 021 488 3710; e reservations@fotaisland.ie; www.fotaisland.ie. 18 holes. 71 par. Visitors welcome. Low season €65–70 (midweek), €85 (weekend). High season €80–105 (midweek), €110 (weekend).

Harbour Point Golf Club Clash Rd, Little Island; ☎ 021 435 3094; e hpoint@iol.ie; www.harbourpointgolfclub.com. 18 holes. 72 par. Length of course: 6,102m (6,712 yards). Visitors welcome. Club professional Morgan O'Donovan provides tuition. €35 (midweek), €40 (weekend). €25 midweek (except Tue) before 11.00.

Kinsale Golf Club Farrangalway, Kinsale; ☎ 021 477 4722; e office@kinsalegolf.com; www.kinsalegolfclub.com. 18 holes (plus a 9-hole course). 71 par. Visitors welcome, booking required at weekends.

Lee Valley Golf and Country Club Clashnure, Ovens; ☎ 021 733 1721; e reservations@leevalleygcc.ie; www.leevalleygcc.ie. 18 holes. 72 par. Length of course: 6,077m (6685 yards). Visitors welcome, booking required at weekends. Club professional John Savage provides tuition. €55 (midweek), €65 (weekend).

Mahon Golf Club Clover Hill, Blackrock; ☎ 021 429 2212, Leisureworld: 021 429 2543; e mahongolfclub@eircom.net (club); www.mahongolfclub.com. 18 holes. 68 par. Visitors welcome (excluding Fri, Sat & Sun afternoon). Reservations made through Leisureworld.

Monkstown Golf Club Parkgariff, Monkstown; ☎ 021 484 1376; e office@monkstowngolfclub.com; www.monkstowngolfclub.com.18 holes. 70 par. Length of course: 5,640m (6,204 yards). Visitors welcome, booking essential. €43 (midweek), €50 (weekend).

Muskerry Golf Club Carrigrohane; ☎ 021 438 5297; f 021 4516 860. 18 holes. 71 par. Length of course: 5754m (6330 yards). Visitors welcome, booking essential.

Old Head Golf Links Kinsale; ☎ 021 477 8444; e info@oldheadgolf.ie; www.oldheadgolflinks.com. 18 holes. 72 par. Length of course: 6,545m (7,200 yards). Visitors welcome, booking essential. €275.

Youghal Golf Club Knockaverry; ✆ 024 92787; ℻ 024 92641; www.youghalgolfclub.com. 18 holes. 70 par. Visitors welcome (excluding Wed).

GREYHOUND RACING
Curraheen Park Greyhound Stadium *Curraheen;* ✆ *021 454 3095 or 1850 525 575;* e *reservations@curraheenpark.igb.ie or crkhospitality@igb.ie for restaurant bookings and information; www.igb.ie; open Wed, Thu & Sat, racing commences at 20.02, doors open at 18.45, 10 races per night; adults* €10, *concessions* €5
No 8 bus from Patrick St. By car – Curraheen is southwest of the city centre, just beyond Wilton. Return journey – courtesy bus every 20mins to city centre 22.30–00.30.
If you are at all partial to the occasional flutter, then a night out at the dogs might be just the ticket. Less than ten minutes' drive from the city centre (get a taxi or the bus if you don't want to drive), is Curraheen Park Greyhound Stadium, where, if you really want to make a night of it, you can enjoy fine dining in the Laurels Restaurant (make a reservation) while experiencing the heart-palpitating thrill of table-side tote betting. You can also watch the race from the bar where they have live music with a different band each night.

HURLING Another native Irish game, it is often referred to as the 'clash of the ash'. Widely recognised as one of the fastest games in the world, it's a rougher version of hockey. Played on the same field as Gaelic football, a small leather-covered ball the size of a baseball and called a *sliotar* (pronounced 'slitter') is passed around the field, amongst a team of 15, using hurleys – ash sticks which are a bit wider at one end. The players can also run with the ball balanced on the hurley for a short distance. The aim of the game is to score points or goals by hitting the *sliotar* between the goalposts. If the ball goes into the net, it's a goal. If the ball goes over the bar, it's a point, and three points are equal to one goal. The Cork team are often referred to as the Blood and Bandages – rather gruesome, but it refers to the Cork colours rather than any propensity on the part of the team for injuring themselves. The Cork colours are red and white, taken from the limestone and red sandstone of the Shandon Steeple.

ROAD BOWLING If, perchance, you have hired a car and are braving Cork's pot-hole-infested backroads, you're unlikely to suddenly find yourself in the middle of a herd of cattle or sheep (as some sentimental films would have you believe is the norm) but you might come across a road-bowling match. Bowling (pronounced like 'howling') is a tough enough game but the rules are relatively simple and very similar to golf. The object is to throw a 28oz cast-iron bowl over one to two miles of a selected public road in the least number of shots. You don't have to get the bowl in a hole at the end, you simply pass a line. This all sounds easy enough, but hurling a heavy bowl at high speed over trees and even houses, spinning it a certain way to account for the bend in the road and desperately trying not to hit any onlookers takes more than a little skill, but this is also what makes the game so thrilling. It's played in a few areas around the country, but primarily in Cork and Armagh. There are even All-Ireland championships.

The fixtures are advertised every Saturday in the *Irish Examiner* and every day during the summer months in the classified section under 'Road bowling'.

GEOGRAPHY AND CLIMATE

Cork is built on a marsh and, like Venice, is actually sinking. This accounts for a certain amount of the dampness likely to be encountered on any trip to Cork. The climate is generally moderate and mild, it is influenced by the warm waters of the Gulf Stream and is in the path of the prevailing southwesterly winds coming from the Atlantic. This means that Ireland is rarely exposed to extremes of weather but it is very changeable. There are several sayings to accompany Ireland's erratic and often frustrating weather: 'We don't have a climate, we just have weather', and the pithier, and I suppose more optimistic 'If you don't like the weather, wait ten minutes'. Average temperatures: winter 7°C, spring and autumn 13°C; summer 18°C. There can be up to 18 hours of daylight during the summer but always, *always*, the possibility of rain; bring an umbrella. In fact, have one surgically attached to your hand. There's nothing worse than stepping out into a downpour only to realise you've lost your umbrella. Visitors should dress in layers to accommodate the rapidly changing weather. Once you are in the country you can tune in to RTÉ Radio I (89FM) for detailed weather forecasts at 06.02, 07.55, 12.53 and 23.55 daily. For area forecasts call 1550 123 + 721 (Munster), 722 (Leinster), 723 (Connacht), 724 (Ulster), 725 (Dublin) or 726 (sea area). Alternatively look up the following websites: www.ireland.com/weather or www.meteireann.ie.

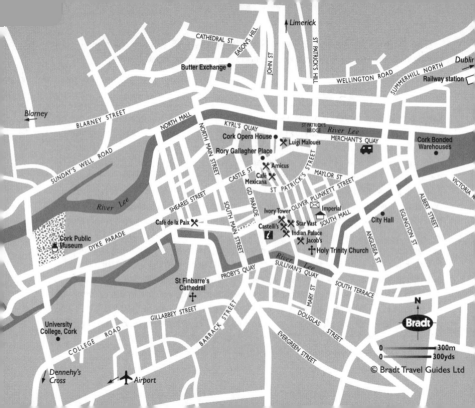

CATHEDRAL ST

EASON'S HILL

↑ Limerick

JOHN ST

ST PATRICK'S HILL

→ Dublin

SUMMERHILL NORTH

WELLINGTON ROAD

Railway station

Butter Exchange ●

Blarney →

BLARNEY STREET

NORTH MALL

KYRL'S QUAY

ST PATRICK'S BRIDGE

River Lee

MERCHANT'S QUAY

Cork Bonded Warehouses

Cork Opera House ●

★ Luigi Maloues

Rory Gallagher Place

NORTH MAIN STREET

SUNDAY'S WELL ROAD

River Lee

★ Amicus

Café Mexicana ✕

CASTLE ST

ST PATRICK'S STREET

MAYLOR ST

GD PARADE

SHEARES STREET

SOUTH MAIN STREET

OLIVER PLUNKETT STREET

Café de la Paix ✕

Ivory Tower ✕

✉ Imperial

ALBERT STREET

EGLINTON ST

VICTORIA N

Cork Public Museum

DYKE PARADE

Castelli's ✕✕ ★ Star Vast

ℹ️ ✕ Indian Palace

Jacob's ✕

SOUTH MALL

City Hall

ANGLESEA ST

✝ Holy Trinity Church

PROBY'S QUAY

River Lee

SULLIVAN'S QUAY

MARY ST

SOUTH TERRACE

St Finbarre's Cathedral ✝

University College, Cork ●

COLLEGE ROAD

GILLABBEY STREET

BARRACK STREET

DOUGLAS STREET

EVERGREEN STREET

N

Bradt

0 ———— 300m
0 ———— 300yds

↓ Dennehy's Cross

✈ Airport

© Bradt Travel Guides Ltd

2 Planning

THE CITY – A PRACTICAL OVERVIEW

Technically the city centre is located on an island, surrounded by two channels of the River Lee and linked to the 'mainland' by numerous bridges. Initially this can be a little confusing for the first-time visitor, especially with all the one-way streets, but the city is so compact that it's usually not long before you get your bearings.

St Patrick's Street, usually referred to simply as Patrick Street, or Pana if you are very local, is the main shopping street where all the usual high-street chains are well represented. It runs from Patrick's Bridge on the south channel of the Lee down to Grand Parade which meets the north channel. St Finbarre's Cathedral is just west over the Nano Nagle Bridge at the end of Grand Parade. There are several pedestrianised side streets running off Patrick Street that also have quite a few smaller and sometimes more interesting shops, as well as a vast range of restaurants. Have a look along French Church Street and Carey's Lane in particular. From Grand Parade you can head west down Washington Street, Lancaster Quay and Western Road where the university lies. Lots of pubs are to be encountered on the way. This is also the direction you need to take to west Cork.

On the north side of the river, again across from Patrick's Bridge, you have

MacCurtain Street running to the east. A busy street with pubs, restaurants and hotels, it is particularly lively during the Jazz Weekend in October as the Metropole Hotel is one of the main venues. The train station is just east of MacCurtain Street, as is the road to Dublin and Rosslare. West of MacCurtain Street is the historic Shandon area (the bells). Northwest of Shandon is Blarney (the stone). The bus station is on the southeast side of Patrick's Bridge.

There are a few things worth bearing in mind if you do get lost and have to ask for directions. Firstly, North Main Street and South Main Street are not neatly intersected by Washington Street (as many people believe). When you are heading west down Washington Street and come to South Main Street on the left, the street to your right is also South Main Street. It becomes North Main Street at the next intersection (Sheares Street to the left, Castle Street to the right). So, for example, if you are looking for the Raven Bar, people may tell you it's on North Main Street but it's actually South Main Street. Secondly, Washington Street is divided into Washington Street and Washington Street West although very few places in the latter will identify themselves as such. Thus, several places appear to have the same address; for example, both the Long Island and Costigan's (bars) have 11 Washington Street as their address, but Costigan's is technically Washington Street West, as is any other address west of the Courthouse.

The last few years have seen a lot of change in Cork city. Mahon Point, a large shopping complex incorporating high street stores, restaurants and cafés, a multiplex cinema and perhaps the biggest lure of all, free parking, has opened up on the ring road near the Jack Lynch Tunnel. This has had a significant impact on business in the city centre but there are plans in motion to counteract this with the development of more shopping centres in the city centre itself. A four-star Clarion Hotel has opened up on the vastly improved Lapp's Quay behind the bus station which now has a very smart boardwalk as well as a few cafés and of course, lots of office space. Lancaster Quay has also been spruced up with a new-look Jury's Hotel. Plans for the building caused controversy initially because it was going to obscure views of St Finbarre's Cathedral, but the final version still allows for a glimpse of the three spires. It's this kind of regeneration which is changing the shape and focus of the city centre. It's an exciting time for Cork although there is, I think, some concern amongst locals about the proliferation of bland but expensive apartment blocks, not to mention the squeezing out of small businesses to make way for corporations. Time will tell if Cork is being rejuvenated with appropriate sensitivity.

There were high hopes for the newly landscaped Patrick Street; traffic was to be one-way only, the idea being that the street would be pedestrianised during business hours, with buses and taxis the only traffic allowed on the city's main thoroughfare. However, while this was a great idea, it wasn't sustainable and traffic is once again two-way, all day. However, a new pedestrian bridge has gone up between Kyrl's Quay and Pope's Quay, thus making access to Shandon easier. At the time of writing Grand Parade was one big construction site and was not a pleasant street to negotiate, but it is being revamped in line with Patrick Street's new look and promises to be a very grand Grand Parade once it's done.

Ireland in general probably gets most of its visitors during the summer months and there is no reason not to visit Cork during that time; it's Cork's peak season too. However, there are plenty of reasons to come here during the more inclement months. Personally I think October is the best time to visit the city. The following is a breakdown of a typical Cork year.

FEBRUARY
Springtime Literature Festival *Munster Literature Centre, Tigh Litríochta, Frank O'Connor House, 84 Douglas St;* ⅋/f *021 431 2955;* e *munsterlit@eircom.net; www.munsterlit.ie* [G4]

An annual four-day festival run by the Munster Literature Centre, it has a different theme every year. Workshops, readings, book launches and masterclasses all focus on the chosen topic. In 2006 they held a Literary Festival of Love and Desire. Venues include the Munster Literature Centre and the Triskel Arts Centre.

MARCH
Cork French Film Festival *Triskel Arts Centre, 14a Tobin St;* ⅂ *021 427 2022;* e *info@triskelartscentre.com; www.triskelartscentre.com* [F3]

Over 18 years old now, the French Film Festival expands every year, including general screenings, family screenings, classics and general education programmes. It usually lasts around two weeks.

St Patrick's Day The River Lee will not run green, nor will the beer, but if the barman has time he might inscribe a little shamrock on the creamy head of your pint. There are parades all over the country on 17 March, a bank holiday, and much revelry in the pubs afterwards. If the weather is pleasant it's a fun day for kids too with lots of street entertainment.

APRIL

Cork International Choral Festival *Civic Trust House, 50 Pope's Quay;* \ *021 421 5125;* e *chorfest@iol.ie; www.corkchoral.ie* [F2]

Running for over 50 years now, the choral festival is held annually over the four days preceding the first Monday in May in Cork's City Hall. One of Europe's premier international choral festivals, it is noted for its high competitive standards, excellent organisation and the friendliness of its welcome. Each year some of the finest international choirs are selected to compete for the prestigious Fleischman International Trophy. The selected choirs also have an opportunity to perform non-competitively in a range of festival activities throughout the weekend. A nightly Festival Club is organised to allow participants to meet informally in a relaxed social setting. The festival also features adult, youth and school choirs who participate in national competitions. Attracting some 5,000 participants, the festival ensures that choral music is brought both to the people of Cork and to the many visitors who travel to the city for the event. Future festival dates: 53rd: 2–6 May 2007; 54th: 30 April–4 May 2008; 55th: 29 April–3 May 2009; 56th: 28 April–2 May 2010; 57th: 27 April–1 May 2011.

Franciscan Well Easter Beer Fest *Franciscan Well, 14 North Mall;* ☎ *021 439 3434;* e *info@franciscanwellbrewery.com; www.franciscanwellbrewery.com* [D2] *(See also Chapter 6, pages 125–6.)*

Technically this may not take place in April, given the variable nature of Easter, but this raucous festival does take place over Easter weekend. With an outdoor heated beer tent to give the transition from winter to spring a bit of a boost, there is a wide selection of unusual Irish beers and ciders as well as an all-day barbecue. Funky tunes add to the festive vibe and you can do it all again in October (see pages 36–7). Admission free.

MAY

Heineken Kinsale Rugby Sevens by the Sea e *info@kinsalesevens.com; www.kinsalesevens.com*

An annual event held during the May Bank Holiday weekend. Kinsale RFC plays host to over 80 teams of varying abilities for a festival of seven-a-side rugby. Played across five pitches, with full hospitality on site at the event, over 150 matches are staged. Always attracts a large number of rugby enthusiasts.

JUNE

Woodford Bourne Cork Midsummer Festival ☎ *021 427 5874;* e *info@ corkfestival.com; www.corkfestival.com*

The Cork Midsummer Festival, originally called A Sense of Cork, was initiated in 1997 by the Lord Mayor of Cork who recognised the city's cultural resurgence and saw the need for a cross-disciplinary festival promoting the arts of Cork, both within the city and beyond. It was also established as the only summer festival in the city and one of the only major cross-arts festivals in the south of the Republic. The festival takes place for 12 days annually, always around the summer solstice.

The festival has grown since its inception and now encompasses all major artistic forms, including dance, theatre, literature, music and visual art, and plays to audiences of around 50,000 annually. While the festival is particularly popular with audiences aged 18–35, the range of programming for all tastes and age groups is increasing and one of the festival's perennial favourites is its family fun day 'Picnic in the Park'. Events in the festival take place in most recognised city venues but the festival also has an enviable record in animating unusual spaces in the city – for example, a puppet show in a museum and a live daily soap opera in the back room of a popular bar.

The festival's greatest strength is its work with many of Cork's strongest artists and arts companies: the two weeks of the festival are a great showcase for much of the best work happening in Cork.

JULY
Soundeye Festival of the Arts of the Word e *festival@soundeye.org;*
www.soundeye.org/festival
A week-long poetry festival held primarily in the Firkin Crane. Poetry readings, performances and discussions.

AUGUST

The Cork Art Fair *www.corkartfair.com*

A newcomer, the Cork Art Fair started in 2005. Held over a weekend in Cork City Hall, it focuses on contemporary art, featuring paintings, sculptures, photographs and prints from artists and galleries both in Ireland and abroad.

SEPTEMBER

Beamish Experience Festival *Beamish & Crawford Plc, South Mail St;* ☎ *021 491 1100;* e *info@beamish.ie; www.beamish.ie*

The 'pub festival with a difference'. A weekend gig trail, with dozens of gigs in dozens of pubs, very much a something-for-everyone experience – rock, roots, comedy, DJs, dance and jazz. Many of the gigs are free of charge, a small cover charge applies for some while the bigger names are ticketed events. Tickets available from Ticketmaster (see *Chapter 3*, page 63).

Beamish Cork Folk Festival *Civic Trust House, 50 Pope's Quay;* ☎ *087 275 9311;* e *corkfolkfestival@oceanfree.net; www.corkfolkfestival.com* [F2]

Normally held in early September (or late August), this is a relaxed festival with plenty of gigs and late-night sets. The festival began in 1979 and its aim is to showcase the very best of both folk and traditional music, song and dance. Over the years folk legends such as Christy Moore, Paul Brady, The Chieftains, Billy Bragg and John Spillane have all performed at this well-established festival. Over 200 musicians, singers and entertainers, local, national and international, gather in Cork for a diverse range of concerts and *céilís*. There is also a free Beamish Pub Trail offering informal music sessions in various pubs around the city centre.

Cape Clear Island International Storytelling Festival *Cape Clear Island, Skibbereen, Co Cork;* e *stories@indigo.ie*

Dates for this hugely popular weekend festival vary from year to year: it can take place any time during September or October. There is a heavy itinerary for the three days (all ticketed events, some of which are free), including storytelling concerts, boat trips, birdwatching walks, archaeological and flora/fauna walks, storytelling workshops, story swaps, bilingual (Irish/English) storytelling, workshops for children, fireside tales, music, focused discussions – all of which attract leading storytellers from around the world as well as aspiring *seanchaís* (traditional Irish storytellers). The rugged beauty of Cape Clear Island provides the perfect inspirational background.

Weekend adult tickets (covering most events) €55, concessions €50. All other single-event tickets €12, concessions €10, children 12 and under €5. Tickets and accommodation should be booked well in advance.

Frank O'Connor International Short Story Festival *Munster Literature Centre, Tigh Litríochta, Frank O'Connor House, 84 Douglas St;* ✆/f *021 431 2955;* e *munsterlit@eircom.net; www.munsterlit.ie* [G4]

The only annual festival in an English-speaking country dedicated to the short story, it is run by the Munster Literature Centre (see *Chapter 10*, pages 181–4) and was first held in 2000. The purpose of the festival is to celebrate the genius of the Cork-born writer Frank O'Connor and in particular the literary form which made him famous the world over. The festival, which lasts about a week and sees several renowned writers – Irish and international – converge on the city, consists of workshops, readings, interviews, films, talks and panel discussions, all of which take place in a number of different venues around the city. On the last night the winner of the Frank O'Connor Short Story Award is announced. Previous winners include Haruki Murakami and Yiyun Li.

Pre-booking highly recommended, no admittance once performances have started. Ticket prices vary, some events are free, some have concessions for students and OAPs.

OCTOBER

Cork Film Festival *Emmet House, Emmet Place;* ↘ *021 427 1711;*
e *info@corkfilmfest.org; www.corkfilmfest.org*
One of Ireland's premier cultural events, the Cork Film Festival celebrated its 50th year in 2005. Attracting an ever-increasing audience of general public, film-lovers and film-makers, the festival has also grown in reputation both nationally and internationally. Naturally enough it is an important showcase for Irish film production, but the week-long programme also includes a diverse range of big-budget movies, world cinema, independent films, documentaries and short films from all over the

globe. The films are shown in several different venues including the Opera House, the Kino, the Triskel, the Gate Multiplex and sometimes even the Farmgate Café in the English Market. The opening and closing films are always shown in the Opera House, after which there is always much revelry in the OH bars. If you are around for a few weeks before the festival (usually held in the second week of October) you may be able to pick up some volunteer work: the bonus here is that you get to see the films for free. The organisers open up a temporary box office a few weeks prior to the festival but its location varies from year to year. The best thing to do is contact the Kino Cinema (see *Chapter 7*, page 136) or look up their website (*www.kinocinema.net*).

Guinness Jazz Festival *Cork Jazz Marketing Association, 20 South Mall;* ✆ *021 427 8979;* e *corkjazz@corkcity.ie; www.guinnessjazzfestival.com*
As many as 40,000 music fans descend on Cork city every October for the Guinness Jazz Festival, reckoned to be Europe's friendliest of its kind. The atmosphere is convivial, the beer free-flowing and the music second to none. As Ireland's most prestigious jazz festival, it's also one of the most important events in the country's cultural calendar, usually held over the bank holiday weekend at the end of October.

Since the birth of the festival in the late 1970s, Cork has played host to many of the jazz greats – Ella Fitzgerald, Dizzy Gillespie, Mel Torme, Dave Brubeck, Chick Corea and countless others. You will find live jazz in over 75 venues in the city, the main events being in the Everyman Palace Theatre, the Cork Opera House and the Triskel Arts Centre. The famous Guinness Festival Club at the Gresham Metropole Hotel offers world-class jazz on five stages, day and night, with the added bonus that the daytime sessions are free; admission is charged after 18.00. Tickets are usually around €20. Everyone winds up in the Metropole at some point and it's probably the best place to go if you're on your own; there's a good buzz, you'll hear plenty of jazz and meet lots of people. Meanwhile the Guinness Jazz Trail offers entertainment in over 40 pubs and clubs – most of which have free entry. Watch out for flyers. Most of the hotels also put on entertainment and for the true fanatic there are usually a few fringe events taking place, including workshops and suchlike. Tickets, which vary in price depending on the artist (generally €20–30), usually go on sale at the beginning of September. Travel and accommodation should also be booked early to avoid disappointment.

Kinsale Fringe Jazz Festival www.kinsale.ie/kinsalejazz.htm

This coincides with the Guinness Jazz Festival (see above) which takes place in Cork city, and is ideal for those who want to enjoy their jazz without the urban chaos. There's jazz all weekend from noon to midnight in the various pubs and hotels around the town, with an emphasis on family events on the Sunday. Seaside setting, fabulous restaurants and if the weather is pleasant this is a nice get-away-from-the-city option.

Franciscan Well October Beer Festival Franciscan Well, 14 North Mall; ℡ 021 439 3434; e info@franciscanwellbrewery.com; www.franciscanwellbrewery.com [D2]

October can be chilly, but with a heated outdoor tent packed with revellers, a barbecue and over 15 foreign draught beers as well as many more bottled beers to choose from, keeping warm shouldn't be a problem for at least one weekend in the month. As well as the numerous foreign beers, the Well also has its own beers on offer as it is also a brewery (see *Chapter 6*, pages 125–6). *Admission free.*

Kinsale Autumn Flavours Festival of Fine Food and Fun *Kinsale Chamber of Tourism, Scilly, Kinsale;* ✆ *021 477 4026;* e *info@kinsale-tourism.ie; www.kinsale.ie*

An important one on the foodies' radar, this is a four-day festival promoted by Kinsale's New Good Food Circle (a collection of restaurants working together) in conjunction with the Kinsale Chamber of Tourism. Starting as early as 09.00, each day it is packed to capacity with different gastronomical, sporting and cultural events. Many events have tickets available at the door. Golf, historical strolls, treasure hunts, wine tastings, brewery tours, harbour cruises, Guinness and oysters, cocktail parties, ghost tours, street entertainment, competitions, Black-Tie Autumn Ball – and all just half-an-hour's drive from Cork city.

NOVEMBER/DECEMBER

Art Trail *Wandesford Quay Studios, Crosses Green;* ✆ *021 496 1449;* e *info@arttrail.ie; www.arttrail.ie* [E3]

Founded in 1996, this two-week art festival provides an innovative and unique platform for Cork-based artists to promote and develop their work. Based around the Backwater Artists Group, which is housed in a renovated mill on Wandesford Quay, the studios therein as well as numerous other studios around the city are opened up to the public for two weeks. A voluntary organisation, Art Trail's ambitious programme includes not just open studios, but also exhibitions, workshops and lectures. Art Trail allows local artists to engage in an open dialogue with guest artists, critics, curators and the general public. Enormously successful every year, it is well worth checking out even if you only have a passing interest in art. It does occasionally occur at other times of the year.

City Hall Crafts Fair *City Hall, Angelsea St* [J3]

With close on 90 stalls exhibiting high-quality handcrafted wares, this is a good place to get in some Christmas shopping. Held every year over one of the first weekends of December, this four-day crafts fair always draws a large crowd. Pottery, clothes, chocolate, soap, candles, ceramics, cheese, art, photography, Celtic designs, batik, knitwear, handbags, and any number of slate/silk/leather/wood/glass goods, it's a great place to pick up some unusual and unique gifts or even just well-deserved treats for yourself. A small café also operates on the premises for the duration of the fair. *Opening hours vary, but open for best part of each day. Admission €5.*

RANDOM
Mind, Body, Spirit Festival *City Hall, Anglesea St* [J3]

This festival used to take place in spring but now appears to occur at varying times of year. If you are interested in coming over for it, the best place to direct your enquiries would probably be Dervish, an alternative shop on Cornmarket Street (see *Chapter 8*, pages 141–2). Festival opening hours vary, but it's open for the best part of each day. Admission is approx €5. A three-day festival, it always draws a large crowd of those interested in all things esoteric. Lots of feature workshops and free lectures covering anything from clinical iridology to connecting with your healing angel guides. There are also over 60 stalls where you can avail yourself of all sorts of demonstrations, have your tarot cards read, and buy anything from crystals to photos of your aura.

SUGGESTED ITINERARIES

ONE DAY

- Ring the Shandon Bells [F1]
- Visit the Cork City Gaol [A2]
- Recuperate with a pint of one of the local stouts in a beer garden and have a pub lunch. Maybe try the tapas at Boqueria. [G2]
- Have a wander around the city centre making sure to include the English Market [F3] and Finbarre's Cathedral [E4]
- Visit the Crawford Art Gallery [F2]
- Have a few drinks in the Crane Lane Theatre [G3] or the more traditional Long Valley [G3]

TWO DAYS

- Ring the Shandon Bells [F1]
- Go on a tour of the Beamish and Crawford Brewery [E3]
- Visit UCC [B4] and the Gaol [A4]
- Have a fabulous dinner somewhere like the Ivory Tower [F3] or Café Paradiso [D3]
- Head to a late bar or a nightclub
- On the second day take a trip out to Fota Wildlife Park and the Queenstown Story in Cobh

THREE DAYS OR MORE All of the above and try to catch some live music too. Cypress Avenue or An Cruiscín Lán for up-and-coming bands, the Spailpín Fánach for traditional music. A trip to Kinsale is also worthwhile.

ℹ TOURIST OFFICES

LOCAL

Cork City Grand Parade; ☏ 021 425 5100; e info@corkkerrytourism.ie; www.corkkerry.ie [F3]. *Open Mon–Fri 09.15–17.15, Sat 09.30–16.30.*
Blarney Town Centre; ☏ 021 438 1624
Kinsale Pier Rd; ☏ 021 477 2234; e kinsaletio@eircom.net

IRISH TOURIST OFFICES ABROAD

Australia Level 5, 36 Carrington St, Sydney NSW 2000; 02 9299 6177; e info@tourismireland.com.au

Canada 2 Bloor St West, Suite 3403, Toronto M4W 3E2; 1800 223 6470; e info.ca@tourismireland.com

France Tourisme Irlandais, 33 rue de Miromesnil, 75008 Paris; 01 7020 0020; e info.fr@tourismireland.com

Germany Irland Information, Gutleutstr 32, 60329 Frankfurt am Main; 069 923 1850; e info.de@tourismireland.com

Italy Turismo Irlandese, Via Santa Maria Segreta 6, 20123 Milan; 02 482 96 060; e informazioni@tourismireland.com

Netherlands Ierland Toerisme, Spuistraat 104, 1012 VA Amsterdam; 020 504 0689; e info@ierland.nl

New Zealand Level 6, 18 Shortland St, Private Bag 92136, Auckland 1; 09 977 2255; e tourism@ireland.co.nz

South Africa c/o Development Promotions, Everite Hse, 7th Floor, 20 De Korte St, Braamfontein 2001, Gauteng; 011 339 4865; e helenf@dpgsa.co.za

UK Ireland Desk, Britain Visitor Centre, 1 Regent St, London SW1Y 4XT; 0800 039 7000; e info.gb@tourismireland.com

USA 345 Park Av, New York, NY 10154; 1800 223 6470; e info@irishtouristboard.com

TOUR OPERATORS

AUSTRALIA

Adventure World Level 20, 141 Walker St, North Sydney, NSW 2060; 02 8913 0755; Perth office: 197 St George's Terr, Perth, WA 6000; 08 9226 4525; www.adventureworld.com.au

Eblana Travel Level 4, 67 Castlereagh St, Sydney NSW 2000; 02 9232 8144

FRANCE Official tourism website of Ireland in French: www.tourismireland.com/fra/index.cfm

Gaéland Ashling 4 Quai des Célestins, 75004 Paris; ☏ 01 4271 4444; e resa@gaeland-ashling.com; www.gaeland-ashling.com
Brittany Ferries ☏ 0825 828 828; www.brittany-ferries.fr

GERMANY
Official tourism website of Ireland in German: www.irland-urlaub.de
Accommodation contact details, car-hire etc: www.irlandreisebuero.de
Last-minute flights and hotels: www.ltur.com/de

UK
Aer Lingus Holidays ☏ 0870 876 5000; www.aerlingus.com
Cresta Holidays ☏ 0870 238 7711; www.crestaholidays.co.uk
Going Places ☏ 0870 400 1290; www.goingplaces.co.uk
Irish Ferries Holidays ☏ 0870 517 1717; e info@irishferries.com (ferry queries & bookings), holidaysinireland@irishferries.co.uk (holiday packages – information & bookings); www.irishferries.com
Leisure Breaks ☏ 0845 458 5200; www.irelandbreaks.co.uk
Saddle Skedaddle ☏ 0191 265 1110; e info@skedaddle.co.uk; www.skedaddle.co.uk. Cycling tours of west Cork & Kerry, starting in Kinsale.
Stena Line Holidays ☏ 0870 574 7474; www.stenaline.co.uk
Trailfinders ☏ 0845 050 5940; www.trailfinders.com

USA

Adventures Abroad ☎ 1 800 665 3998; www.adventures-abroad.com

Brian Moore International Tours ☎ 1 800 982 2299; e info@bmit.com; www.bmit.com

CIE International Tours ☎ 1 800 CIE TOUR or 973 292 3438; e reservations@cietours.com;
www.cietours.com

Destinations Ireland ☎ 1 800 832 1848; www.destinations-ireland.com

Euro-Bike & Walking Tours ☎ 1 800 321 6060; www.eurobike.com. Cycling tours of west Cork & Kerry.

Garber Travel ☎ 1 800 FLY GARBER; e info@garbertravel.com; www.garbertravel.com

Irish American International Tours ☎ 1 800 633 0505; www.ireland411.com

Kenny Tours ☎ 1 800 648 1492; e info@kenny-tours.com; www.kenny-tours.com

STA Travel ☎ 1 800 781 4040; www.statravel.com. Travel organisation aimed at students.

RED TAPE

Citizens from certain countries require visas to enter Ireland regardless of the purpose of their trip. Others may need them if they are coming here to work or to spend an extended period of time here. Ideally you should check with the Irish Embassy in the country in which you reside; they will provide you with all the necessary information regarding your entry and stay in Ireland. No visas are required by EU citizens or those from other Western countries such as the US, Canada, Australia and New Zealand.

EMBASSIES

Australia 20 Arkana St, Yarralumla, Canberra, ACT 2600; ✆ 02 6273 3022; e irishemb@cyberone.com.au

Canada 130 Albert St, Suite 1105, Ottawa, Ontario KIP 5G4; ✆ 613 233 6281; e ottowaembassy@dfa.ie

France 4 Rue de Paris, 75116 Paris; ✆ 01 4417 6700; e paris@dfa.ie

Germany Friedrichstr 200, 10117 Berlin; ✆ 030 220 720; f 030 220 72299; www.botschaft-irland.de

Italy Piazza di Campitelli 3, 00186 Rome; ✆ 06 697 9121; f 06 679 2354; www.ambasciata-irlanda.it

Netherlands Dr Kuyperstraat 9, 2514 BA, The Hague; ✆ 070 363 0993; e info@irishembassy.nl; www.irishembassy.nl

Poland ul Mysia 5, 00-496 Warsaw; ✆ 022 849 6633/55; e ambassada@irlandia.pl; www.irlandia.pl

South Africa 1st Floor, Southern Life Plaza, 1059 Schoeman St, Arcadia 0083, Pretoria; ✆ 012 342 5062; e pretoria@dfa.ie; www.embassyireland.org.za

Spain Ireland House, Paseo de la Castellana 46-4, 28046 Madrid; ✆ 091 436 4093; e embajada@irlanda.es

UK 17 Grosvenor Pl, London SW1X 7HR; ✆ 020 7235 2171; f 020 7245 6961

USA 2234 Massachusetts Av, NW Washington, DC 20008; ✆ 202 462 3939; e washingtonembassy@dfa.ie; www.irelandemb.org

CONSULATES

Boston Chase Building, 535 Boylston St, Boston, MA 02116; ✆ 617 267 9330; e irlcons@aol.com

Chicago 400 N Michigan Av, Chicago, IL 60611; ✆ 312 337 1868; e hibernia@interaccess.com

New York Ireland Hse, 345 Park Av, 17th Floor, New York, NY 10154-0037; ✆ 212 319 2555; e congenny@aol.com

New Zealand Level 7, Citibank Bldg, 23 Customs St East, Auckland, New Zealand; ✆ 09 977 2252; e consul@ireland.co.nz

San Francisco 100 Pine St, 33rd Floor, San Francisco, CA 94111; ✆ 415 392 4214; f 415 392 0885

GETTING THERE AND AWAY

✈ BY AIR

Cork Airport Airport code: ORK; ✎ 021 4313131; www.corkairport.com. A large modern new airport only 8km west of the city centre. You can hire a car from there or get either the bus or a taxi into town.

Aer Arann ✎ 0800 587 2324; www.aerarann.com. Flights from Belfast City, Bristol, Cardiff, Edinburgh, Leeds Bradford, Newquay Cornwall & Southampton to Cork.

Aer Lingus ✎ 01 8868844 (Ireland), 0845 973 7747 (UK); www.aerlingus.com. The country's national airline has several direct flights to Cork from the UK & mainland Europe, including Alicante, Amsterdam, Barcelona, London Heathrow, Malaga, Milan (MXP) & Paris (CDG). If you have access to a television once in Ireland, you can check flight information on Aertel page 573.

BMI Baby ✎ 0870 264 2229; www.bmibaby.com. Flights from Birmingham, Leeds Bradford & Manchester to Cork.

British Airways ✎ 0870 850 9850; www.ba.com. Flights from Glasgow & Manchester to Cork.

Jet2.com www.jet2.com. Flights from Newcastle to Cork.

Ryanair ✎ 01 6097800 (Ireland), 0541 569569 (UK); www.ryanair.com. Ireland's low-cost airline flies from London Stansted, Gatwick & Liverpoool to Cork.

🚢 BY CAR/FERRY

Brittany Ferries ✎ 021 427 7801, 0870 411 1199 (Ireland), 0870 536 0360 (UK), 0825 828828 (France); www.brittanyferries.com. Roscoff–Cork, crosses once a week, each way; crossing time of up to 13hrs.

Stena Line ✎ 021 4272965 (Ireland), 0870 570 7070 (UK); www.stenaline.ie. Fishguard–Rosslare Harbour, 4 crossings per day, each way; 3$\frac{1}{2}$hrs with Superferry, Express crossing time 2hrs.

Irish Ferries ☎ 0818 300 400 or 01 661 0511 (Ireland), 0870 517 1717 (UK), 02 9861 1717 (Roscoff), 02 3323 4444 (Cherbourg); www.irishferries.com. Pembroke–Rosslare Harbour, cruise ferry, 2 departures daily in each direction; crossing time 3¾hrs. Cherbourg & Roscoff to Rosslare Harbour; crossing time 18hrs. Cherbourg to Rosslare is the more plied route, generally crossing every second day in the high season. If you book your car trip online, you may get a discount.

Swansea Cork Ferries ☎ 021 483 6000 (Ireland), 0179 245 6116 (UK); www.swanseacorkferries.com. Swansea (or Pembroke, depending on tidal conditions) to Cork; crossing time of 10hrs (8 from Pembroke). Daily crossings in the high season.

After the crossing

It takes about three hours to drive the 206km from Rosslare to Cork. Follow the N25 or signs for New Ross–Waterford–Cork. If you are heading to west Cork (from Dublin or Rosslare) and want to bypass the city, follow signs for the Jack Lynch Tunnel (or for west Cork) at the Dunkettle Roundabout. Ferries arriving in Cork berth in Ringaskiddy, 18km southeast of the city centre.

If you want to break the journey, New Ross is approximately 40 minutes' drive from Rosslare and approx 2½ hours from Cork. The Kennedys hailed from New Ross originally and as such there are a few places worth visiting. If you want to spend the night, I recommend **Killarney House Bed & Breakfast** (*The Maudlins, New Ross, Co Wexford;* ☎ *051 421062; http://homepage.eircom.net/~killarneyhouse*): tranquil setting, complimentary tea/coffee on arrival and an excellent breakfast menu.

Driving in Ireland

Vehicles are driven on the left side of the road. There are five speed limits in place: 50km/h (30mph) in built-up areas, 100km/h (60mph) on all national roads including dual carriageways, 80km/h (50mph) on regional and local roads (also called non-national roads) and 120km/h (75mph) on motorways. Cars on a roundabout (traffic rotary) have a right of way over those entering the roundabout. By law, the driver and all passengers must wear a safety belt. Children under 12 are not allowed to sit in the front. An alcohol limit of 0.08% is strictly enforced. It is illegal to drive while using a hand-held mobile phone. A penalty-points system has been in operation since 2003 and covers a wide range of traffic violations. There is an on-the-spot fine of €80 for speeding offences. Road distances and speed limits are measured in kilometres although there are still some old black and white signs which give distances in miles. The more modern signs are green. (See Chapter 4, *Local transport*, page 68, for further information on car hire.)

Driving in Cork is confusing: there are a lot of one-way streets and seemingly unending roadworks further complicate matters. If your accommodation is quite central, I would recommend walking into the city and just using the car for day trips or for continuing on your journey.

BY TRAIN
From Dublin

Iarnród Éireann Heuston Station, Dublin 8; ☎ 01 771871; www.iarnrodeireann.ie or www.irishrail.ie. Iarnród Éireann (translates as Iron Road of Ireland) is the national railway operator. There are regular trains from Dublin to Cork. Journey time approx 2½–3hrs.

🚌 BY BUS

Eurolines 52 Grosvenor Gdns, Victoria, London SW1W 0AU; ☎ 08705 143219 (central reservations), 01582 404511 (Luton, national call rate), 08705 808080 (rest of Britain, national call rate); e info@buseireann.ie; www.buseireann.ie. London (Victoria) to Cork (Parnell Place) takes 15–18hrs. They sometimes offer discounts on tickets bought online.

From Dublin

Bus Éireann Busáras, Store St; ☎ 01 8366111; www.buseireann.ie. Bus Éireann (translates as Bus of Ireland) is the state company which operates the nationwide bus network. There are regular buses from Busáras to Cork. Journey time approx 4½hrs.

Aircoach ☎ 01 8447118, 0870 225755 (UK); www.aircoach.ie. Aircoach operate a service between Dublin Airport & Dublin city, but they also operate the cheapest bus service between Dublin & Cork. Pick up is at Boyle Sports Shop on Westmoreland Street in Dublin, & the set-down point is the back of the Metropole Hotel on Patrick's Quay in Cork.

From Shannon

Bus Éireann Operate a service between Shannon Airport & Cork. Journey time approx 2½hrs.

🕒 TIME

From the end of October to the end of March, Ireland is on Greenwich Mean Time. From the end of March to the end of October it changes to GMT plus one hour.

✚ HEALTH AND SAFETY with Dr Felicity Nicholson

The EHIC (European Health Insurance Card) has replaced the E111 form and should be brought with you if you are an EU citizen; it will cover you for most medical care. The card is available free of charge (☎ *0845 606 2030; www.ehic.org.uk*) and is valid for five years. It is recommended that non-EU citizens take out health insurance. There are no inoculations required for entry into the country. However, if in the previous fortnight you have been in a country where a contagious disease is prevalent, proof of immunisation may be required. Don't bring food into the country.

The streets of Cork can be an unpleasant place to be once the pubs have closed. Don't hang around, avoid dimly lit streets and get a cab if you have any distance to go.

TRAVEL CLINICS AND HEALTH INFORMATION A full list of current travel clinic websites worldwide is available on www.istm.org. For other journey preparation information, consult www.tripprep.com. Information about various medications may be found on www.emedicine.com/wild/topiclist.htm.

🎒 WHAT TO TAKE

There's not much that you absolutely need to take. Most essentials are readily available so there's no panic if you forget something. I would suggest bringing what you need from home, however, as it's probably cheaper there. Do bring an umbrella and walking shoes. If you're coming sometime other than summer, I would recommend a good raincoat. On the flipside, if you are coming in summer, bring a decent pair of sunglasses and sunscreen. You may also need a plug adaptor. Electricity in Ireland is 220 volts: appliances use three-pin plugs. US appliances operate at 110–120 volts so you may need a transformer to prevent damage. I would also suggest sending yourself an email with your passport number and the contact details of your local bank at home in case of misplaced cards.

$ MONEY AND BUDGETING

CURRENCY The Republic of Ireland is part of the Eurozone and the euro is the only currency accepted there. For visitors coming from the States, at the time of writing the euro was worth about US$1.25 (£0.67). American $100 bills won't be cashed, so bring smaller denominations or get your euro before you go. In English, the euro is generally written and spoken of in the singular, for example five euro, twenty cent; not five euros, twenty cents. Notes are valued at €5, €10, €20, €50, €100, €200 and €500. Many places may have difficulty in changing any of the last three so it's advisable to concentrate on the lower values. Coins are valued at 1c, 2c, 5c (all copper), 10c, 20c, 50c (all gold), €1 and €2 (a mix of gold and silver). The notes are the same regardless of their country of origin: all feature architectural images. All the coins have a map of Europe on one

NO SMOKING

As of 29 March 2004 it has been illegal to smoke in the workplace in Ireland. This includes pubs, nightclubs, restaurants, cafés and, somewhat controversially, company cars. This government smoking ban is meant to control the effects of passive smoking. EU-funded research had been carried out on powerful ventilation systems and it was shown that even these could not clear pub air of the harmful substances contained in tobacco smoke. Many welcomed the ban while many more felt it was a blow to their freedom. By and large, however, it has been a great success. Most pubs now offer outdoor seating either in front of the pub or in the form of a beer garden. There are also some pubs which have 'smoking rooms'.

side, while the reverse design depends on where the coin was minted: Irish coins feature a harp. Regardless of the image, all the notes and coins can be used in any Eurozone country.

BUDGETING There's no getting away from the fact that Ireland is not a cheap place to visit. Luckily Cork is a student city and so good times can certainly be had without breaking the bank. If, however, money is not an issue, believe me, you will have no problem spending it.

Rock bottom

€*30 a day* If you stay in a hostel, where you can potentially cook all your own meals if necessary, accommodation need only cost you about €15 a night. Have a large lunch in the late afternoon for about €10 and spend your time window-shopping, visiting the free sights (all the art galleries are free) and maybe treat yourself to a pint in the evening in a pub with free live music.

Modest

€*100 a day* Stay in a cheaper bed and breakfast, enjoy a reasonably priced lunch and an 'Early Bird Menu' in the evening, catch some sights and have a few drinks.

Fun

€*200 a day* Splash out on a posher bed and breakfast, somewhere on the Western Road so you can still walk into town. For €50 you'll get a nice room with a good breakfast. You can have a reasonably priced lunch in town and then dinner in a good restaurant. You'll be able to see a few sights, maybe get in a day trip to somewhere like Cobh and enjoy an evening out.

Extravagant

€*500 a day* You can stay in a luxury hotel, eat all your meals out in Cork's top restaurants, shop and sightsee all you like, take in some theatre or concerts, spend some time somewhere like Kinsale, availing yourself of all the gourmet food on offer.

3 Practicalities

BANKS AND MONEY MATTERS

BANKS AND ATMS There are branches all over the city centre, with several along Patrick Street and the South Mall. Opening hours are usually Monday–Friday 10.00–16.00, depending on the bank. There are dozens of ATMs around the city, and not just at the banks. Many of the shopping centres, supermarkets and department stores have ATMs on their premises. If you have a PIN (personal identification number) you can make cash withdrawals from the ATMs using your credit card (although this can be quite expensive) and usually with any card with a Cirrus, Maestro, Link or Plus logo.

CURRENCY EXCHANGE Available at the airport, banks, the city centre tourist office and post offices. The best exchange rate is at the banks.

THE EURO See *Money and budgeting*, pages 50–1.

CREDIT AND DEBIT CARDS Visa and MasterCard are widely accepted, American Express and Diners Club not so widely. Switch is not accepted. If you lose your cards it is advisable to cancel them straight away. The best thing to do is to contact your own branch directly (which you will need to do anyway regarding American Express and Diners), so bring the contact details with you. Failing that you can call Visa (✆ 1800 558002) and MasterCard (✆ 1800 557378) direct.

TRAVELLERS' CHEQUES Travellers' cheques are really only useful for those travelling from outside the Eurozone, although credit cards and ATM cards are probably an easier way to gain access to your money. Thomas Cook, American Express and Visa are all readily accepted and can be cashed in banks but there will be a commission charge. American Express cheques can also be cashed in the tourist office on Grand Parade.

CUSTOMS AND VALUE ADDED TAX Visitors from EU countries do not have to make a declaration to customs provided the goods imported are not for commercial purposes. No duty or tax has to be paid on alcohol or cigarettes if the quantity can be reasonably assumed to be for personal use. Visitors from outside the EU are subject to tighter restrictions. Visitors from Britain may bring their pet cats and dogs into the country; all other visitors will have to apply for a pet passport. See www.irlgov.ie/daff or www.revenue.ie for more details.

Visitors from non-EU countries can obtain a refund of the value added tax (VAT) on any of the relevant goods they have bought in the two months prior to their leaving the Republic. A sales tax of 20% is applied to most goods, so it is worth enquiring in the shop, before making a purchase, whether or not they are participants in the Retail Export Scheme. The money is refunded to you at either Dublin or Shannon airport. There is no VAT on books or children's shoes.

C COMMUNICATIONS

TELEPHONES Eircom is the country's largest service provider. If you are using public phones Eircom are the best value. Minimum charge is 50c. Alternatively you can buy phonecards available at most newsagents. Most public phones will accept both coin and card. Calls are cheaper at the weekend and after 18.00 Monday–Friday. If you are phoning abroad, however, a call shop is probably the most comfortable and most cost-effective option. There are dozens all over the city. Most internet cafés double as call shops.

Log on to www.budgetcom.ie for information on cheap calls from Ireland to other countries in western Europe.

Useful telephone numbers

Ambulance ☎ 999

Car pound ☎ 021 430 2222 (€160 to have car released)

SouthDoc (After-hours family doctor service) ☎ 1850 335 999. *Available Mon–Thu 18.00–08.00, Fri 18.00–Mon 08.00 (24hrs at weekends)*

Fire ☎ 999

Directory enquiries ☎ 11811

Police (emergency) ☎ 999; (all other matters) Anglesea St; ☎ 021 431 3031; Bridewell, Cole Quay; ☎ 021 427 0681

Weather forecasts (see *Geography and climate*, page 23)

€ INTERNET AND CALL SHOPS

Internet Exchange 10 Paul St, Rory Gallagher Pl; ☎ 021 485 1546; e iecork@iemail.com [F2] Minimum of €1 per visit. Downloading. *Open Mon–Sun 09.00–22.00.*

Internet Exchange 5 Woods St (off Washington St); ☎ 021 425 4666 [D3] Prices same as above. *Open Mon–Sun 09.00–midnight.*

Fone Home French Church St; ☎ 021 425 4237 [F2] €2 per hr, minimum of €1 per visit. *Open Mon–Sat 10.00–22.00, Sun 10.00–23.00.*

webworkhouse.com 8a Winthrop St; ☎ 021 427 3090; e webworkhouse@wwhmail.com; www.webworkhouse.com [G3] Hourly rates depend on the time of day. 03.00–08.00 €1.50, 08.00–17.00 €3, 17.00–03.00 €2.50. Multi-player online games & 24hr call shop. Also has Western Union money transfer facility. *Open 24hrs.*

Wired to the World 27 Washington St; ☎ 021 480 2560; e wiredtotheworld@gmail.com; www.wiredtotheworld.ie [E3] Internet, gaming & call shop. €2 per hour, €5 for 4hrs, or €10 for the whole day. Minimum of €1.00 for 30 mins. Spend can include internet, phone calls, printing etc. Loyalty card – one free hour internet access with every 5 visits. *Open daily 10.00–midnight.*

Wired to the World 28 North Main St; details & prices same as above [E2] *Open daily 08.00–midnight.*

Wired to the World Thompson Hse, MacCurtain St (opposite 4 Star Pizza) [H2] Largest call shop in Ireland. Gaming & loyalty cards. Prices same as above. *Open Mon–Sat 09.00–midnight, Sun 10.00–midnight.*

✉ POST OFFICES

GPO (General Post Office) Oliver Plunkett St; ℡ 021 4851042; www.anpost.ie [G3] *Open Mon–Sat 09.00–17.30.*
Grand Parade Post Office Grand Parade; ℡ 021 4273645 [F3] *Open Mon–Fri 09.00–13.00, 14.00–17.30.*

MEDIA

PRESS UK daily papers are widely available. Many European publications as well as regional and national Irish newspapers and other publications, as listed below, are readily available from Eason's on Patrick Street (see page 143).

Irish Examiner www.irishexaminer.com. Cork-based national daily.
The Irish Times www.ireland.com. Daily national.
The Irish Independent Daily national.
Evening Echo www.eveningecho.ie. Local evening paper, Mon–Fri.
Corklife www.corklife.ie. Free bi-monthly magazine with all the latest on Cork fashion & beauty, shopping, nightlife, competitions etc. Usually available in bars & restaurants.
WhazOn? www.whazon.com. Free monthly leaflet listing all the latest in arts, entertainment, pubs, restaurants etc.
Totally Cork Free monthly paper with news, reviews & interviews.

TELEVISION RTÉ (Raidió Teilifís Éireann – radio and television of Ireland) is the nation's state-funded television network and operates two channels, RTÉ 1 and RTÉ 2. There are two other stations, TV3, which is purely commercial and TG4, the all-Irish (language) station. Every household has these four stations, and many just these four. However, many more have all the usual British channels as well as satellite and cable television. All the Irish channels are relatively conservative and the focus is largely on light entertainment, with many imported sitcoms, soap operas and dramas from the US and the UK. *Fair City* is the token Irish soap opera in English and *Ros na Rún* is the wonderfully melodramatic Irish-language offering. There are plenty of news programmes and news updates on all channels also.

RADIO There are plenty of radio stations to choose from. Radio 1 (88–90FM, or 252LW) and 2FM (90–92FM) are the two RTÉ stations, the former concentrating on news, analysis and chat shows, the latter on chart music and light entertainment. TodayFM (100–103FM) is a popular rival for 2FM and Lyric FM (96–99FM) is a classical music station. The most popular Cork stations are Cork 96FM and RedFM (104–106FM). Raidió na Gaeltachta (94FM) is the all-Irish radio channel.

Ⓔ EMBASSIES AND CONSULATES

The following diplomatic offices are in Dublin; there are none in Cork, but that doesn't mean they are not accessible.

Australia 7th Floor, Fitzwilton Hse, Wilton Terr, Dublin 2; ☎ 01 664 5300; e austremb.dublin@dfat.gov.au; www.australianembassy.ie

Canada 4th Floor, 65–8 St Stephen's Green, Dublin 2; ☎ 01 417 4100; e dubln@international.gc.ca
France 36 Aylesbury Rd, Ballsbridge, Dublin 4; ☎ 01 277 5000; e chancellerie@ambafrance.ie
Germany 31 Trimleston Av, Booterstown, Co Dublin; ☎ 01 269 3011; e germany@indigo.ie
Italy 63-5 Northumberland Rd, Ballsbridge, Dublin 4; ☎ 01 660 1744; e info@italianembassy.ie
Netherlands 160 Merrion Rd, Ballsbridge, Dublin 4; ☎ 01 269 3444; e info@netherlandsembassy.ie
Poland 5 Aylesbury Rd, Ballsbridge, Dublin 4; ☎ 01 283 0855; e polembas@iol.ie
South Africa 2nd Floor, Alexandra Hse, Earlsfort Terr, Dublin 2; ☎ 01 661 5553; e information@saedublin.com
Spain 17a Merlyn Pk, Ballsbridge, Dublin 4; ☎ 01 283 9900/01; e embespie@mail.mae.es
UK 29 Merrion Rd, Ballsbridge, Dublin 4; ☎ 01 205 3700; e britishembassy@abtran.com; www.britishembassy.ie
USA 42 Elgin Rd, Ballsbridge, Dublin 4; ☎ 01 668 8777; e webmasterireland@state.gov

➕ MEDICAL SERVICES

HOSPITALS
Cork University Hospital Wilton; ☎ 021 454 6400
Mercy University Hospital Grenville Pl; ☎ 021 427 1971 [D3]

PHARMACIES Pharmacies are easily identified by their green-cross sign and most are open usual shopping hours. Some pharmacies have late opening hours.

Phelan's Pharmacy 9 St Patrick's St; ☎ 021 427 2511 [G2] *Open Mon–Fri 08.30–22.00, Sat 09.00–22.00, Sun 10.00–22.00, bank holidays 10.00–18.00.*

Travel Vaccination Centre 9 St Patrick's St (over Phelan's Pharmacy); ☎ 021 427 8699 [G2]. Vaccinations should be administered a month before entering the relevant country. If you find yourself in Cork a month before your departure to a country where vaccinations are required, you can get them by appointment here. *Open Mon–Fri.*

RELIGIOUS SERVICES

There are numerous places of worship in Cork city. Religious services for most denominations are held on Sundays between 10.00 and 12.00. To check the location of a particular church, check the phone book (available for reference in any post office).

LOCAL TOUR OPERATORS

Bus Éireann Parnell Pl; ☎ 021 4508188, (tourist office) 021 425 5100; e info@buseireann.ie; www.buseireann.ie [H2]. Running May–Sep, Bus Éireann have quite a few day trips including an open-top tour of Cork city & Blarney, & a few trips to Kerry, west Cork & Clare. Ticket prices vary. There is a family ticket which will cover one or two adults & up to three children (must be under 16 years of age) & group rates are available on request. All tours depart from the bus station at Parnell Place but some tours may be joined at Blarney or Macroom.

Easy Tours ☎/f 021 434 5328; e info@easytourscork.com; www.easytourscork.com. Operating April–Sep, Easy Tours run several different day trips, including Fota & Blarney, Jameson Distillery, Cobh & Barryscourt Castle, an Atlantic coast drive & west Cork highlights. Tours last 6–8hrs. Ticket prices vary. Pick-up will be at a point convenient to your accommodation. Pre-booking essential. Each trip runs no more than twice a week.

Road Runners West Cork Tours Ltd, New Mill Apts, Kinsale, Co Cork; ☎ 021 477 3423; e westcorktours@eircom.net; www.westcorktours.com. Road Runners operate daily guided tours around Blarney, Kinsale & east Cork. They also run a shore fishing trip, an historic antiquities tour & a tour of private gardens in the Cork area. Daily pick-up & drop-off by arrangement from all hotels & hostels in Cork city & Kinsale, usually between 09.00 & 09.30, returning to Cork city at approximately 17.00. Adults €35, concessions €25, children €20. Ticket prices include entrance fees.

GUIDED TOURS
OLGA (Official Local Guiding Association) Walking Tours *Approved Bord Fáilte Tour Guides;* ☎ *021 477 5405 or* ☎f *021 429 1649;* e *noreenmurphysheehan@eircom.nt*
As well as walking tours, they also do coach tours and have guides who specialise in gardens, historical buildings and sites, golf groups, Irish culture (music, dancing, singing), and hill walking.

The **Historic Cork** tour covers St Finbarre's 7th-century monastic settlement to Viking invasions and Norman influences; a retracing of the old waterways; the Huguenot Quarter; and the English Market. The tour finishes with complimentary tea/coffee in the Cork Vision Centre. Departs from the tourist office on Grand Parade; Wednesday 10.00 mid Jun–mid September; €7 per person; duration approximately 90 minutes.

Take a stroll through the streets on the **Literary Cork** tour. Explore the city of Frank O'Connor, described by W B Yeats as Ireland's answer to Chekhov. Learn more about Cork's connections with James Joyce, Edmund Spenser and Charles

Dickens. Hear about Seán O'Faoláin and why he did not want to accept the freedom of his native city. The tour finishes with a complimentary pint of Beamish Stout or tea/coffee in the city centre pub An Spailpín Fánach.

Departs from the tourist office on Grand Parade; Tuesday and Thursday 19.00 Jun–mid September; €7 per person; duration approximately 90 minutes.

Cork City Tour Bus *Tourist Office, Grand Parade;* ☎ *021 425 5100. Information also available from Cronin's Coaches,* ☎ *021 4309090* [F3]

The open-top bus is always a nice easy way to see any city, especially if the weather is pleasant. The tour takes about an hour and the ticket is valid all day; you can get on and off as often as you wish. Highlights include Cork City Gaol, City Library, St Finbarre's Cathedral, Crawford Municipal Art Gallery, Triskel Art Centre, English Market, Fitzgerald's Park and Cork Public Museum, Cork Opera House, Custom House, Elizabeth Fort, the Courthouse and City Hall.

Tours depart from the City Library on Grand Parade every 45 minutes (Jul–Aug every 30 mins). First tour commences at 09.30, last tour at 17.00. A timetable of other pick-up/set-down points is available from the tourist office. Tours operate daily April–October. Adults €12, concessions €10, children under 14 €4, under 5s free, family ticket (2 adults and up to 4 children) €28. Group rates available on request.

Cork Harbour Cruises *Marine Transport Services, Cobh;* ☎ *021 481 1485*

Educational cruises in Cork Harbour taking in various places of interest. All charters can be arranged from various points in the harbour. Daily harbour cruises from Cobh, June–September, four times daily.

OTHER PRACTICALITIES

DRY CLEANING/LAUNDERETTE

Duds & Suds 1–3 Marybank, Douglas St; ☎ 021 431 4799. *Open Mon–Fri 08.00–21.00, Sat 08.00–18.00.*

LEFT LUGGAGE

Bus Éireann Parnell Pl; ☎ 021 450 8188; e info@buseireann.ie; www.buseireann.ie [H2] The bus station left luggage office is open Mon–Fri 07.45-19.00, Sat 09.00–18.00, Sun 09.00–18.00 (summer only). €2.60 per item for the first day; €2.00 for each subsequent day for up to a month. Uncollected items are disposed of after a month.

TICKETMASTER OUTLETS

Ticketmaster ☎ 0818 719 300; www.ticketmaster.ie
Pro Musica 20 Oliver Plunkett St; ☎ 021 427 1659 [H3]
Ticketron Ground Floor, Merchant's Quay Shopping Centre, 1–5 Patrick St; ☎ 021 427 1100 [G2]

4 Local Transport

🚌 BUSES

CITY BUSES City buses are operated by **Bus Éireann** (*Parnell Pl; ☎ 021 450 8188 (travel centre), 021 422 2129 (talking timetable);* e *info@buseireann.ie; www.buseireann.ie*). Depending on the time of day, bus regularity can be anything from every ten minutes to once an hour. Timetables are readily available from the bus station at Parnell Place but don't rely on them too much; Cork city buses are not known for their punctuality. Standards fall even further when the weather is bad. At rush hour in the evening scheduled buses will often pass you by because they are too full to let any more people on. Local fares: adults € 1.20, children 65c.

City bus routes
Number 1 (Northside Orbital Service) Mayfield–Bishopstown
Number 2 (Northbound) Merchant's Quay–Knocknaheeny
Number 2 (Southbound) Parnell Pl–Mahon
Number 3 Patrick St–Ballyphehane/Farranree
Number 5 Patrick St–Rossa Av/Cork Institute of Technology
Number 6 South Mall–Grange (Douglas)

Number 7 Patrick St–Donnybrook/Ballyvolane
Number 8 (Southbound) Patrick St–Bishopstown
Number 8 (Northbound) Patrick St–Mayfield
Number 10 Grand Parade–Glasheen
Number 10 Grand Parade–Skehard
Number 14 Patrick St–Wilton Shopping Centre/Cork University Hospital
Number 19 Mahon–Douglas–Bishopstown
Number 246 Parnell Pl–Glanmire–Sarsfield Court

Cork county bus routes
Number 223 Parnell Pl–Monkstown–Ringaskiddy–Haulbowline
Number 224 Parnell Pl–Blarney
Number 249 Parnell Pl–Cork Airport–Kinsale–Garrettstown
Number 260 Parnell Pl–Youghal–Ardmore

Nationwide bus routes
Number 8 Parnell Pl–Dublin
Number 40 Parnell Pl–Waterford–Rosslare
Number 40 Parnell Pl–Killarney
Number 51 Parnell Pl–Limerick–Galway

Aircoach (↘ *01 844 7118 (Ireland), 0870 225 755 (UK); www.aircoach.ie*) operate a service between Dublin Airport and Dublin city, but they also operate the cheapest bus service between Dublin and Cork. Pick up is at Boyle Sports Shop on Westmoreland Street in Dublin, and the set-down point is the back of the Metropole Hotel on Patrick's Quay in Cork.

▰▰ TRAINS

Iarnród Éireann/Irish Rail *Kent Station, Lower Glanmire Road;* ➘ *021 4506766 or 1850 366222;* f *021 4505211; www.cie.ie* [K1]
Main train routes are: Cork–Mallow–Dublin, Cork–Cobh and Cork–Tralee.

🚗 TAXIS AND CABS

There are numerous taxi and cab companies within the city and they are usually fairly plentiful when pubs and clubs are closing. Taxis can be hailed on the street, cabs cannot. They don't really differ in price. Taxis have signs on the roof, cabs don't: the latter are identifiable by their yellow plates saying 'hackney'. There is a taxi rank at the bus station at Parnell Place and also at a few locations along Patrick Street – on both sides of the street outside Marks & Spencer, outside Dunnes Stores (northbound) and outside Porter's newsagents (southbound).

Cork Taxi Co-Op 6 Washington St West; ➘ 021 427 2222; www.corktaxicoop.ie [E3]
Lee Cabs North Gate Bridge; ➘ 021 439 3977 [E2]

Wilton Cabs Wilton Shopping Centre; ☎ 021 434 6666
Yellow Cabs 3 Courthouse St (off Washington St); ☎ 021 427 2255 or 021 487 4444 [E3]

✈ AIRPORT TRANSFER

BUS

Air Coach Service (Bus Éireann) ☎ 021 450 8188; e info@buseireann.ie; www.buseireann.ie. Journey time approx 25 mins; tickets €3.80 single, €4.90 day return, €6.30 monthly return. Departs from the bus station at Parnell Place to the airport & back again. There are two or three buses an hour for most of the day. First bus from the airport Mon–Sat 07.50; Sun & public holidays 07.50 Apr–Sep; 12.00 Sep–Mar. Last bus Mon–Fri 21.30; Sat–Sun & public holidays 20.45. First bus from Cork city Mon–Sat 07.30; Sun & public holidays 07.30 Apr–Sep; 11.30 Sep–Mar. Last bus Mon–Fri 21.00; Sat–Sun & public holidays 20.25. Check website for changes to schedule or ticket prices.

The number 249 bus route serves Kinsale & Garrettstown via the airport. First bus from the airport Mon–Sat 08.56; Sun 11.00. Last bus Mon–Sat 23.12; Sun 19.32. First bus from Cork city (Parnell Place) Mon–Sat 07.20; Sun 09.30. Last bus Mon–Sat 22.00, Sun 18.00.

Skylink ☎ 021 432 1020; e info@skylinkcork.com; www.skylinkcork.com. Shuttle service operating between the airport & the city centre, stopping at most city centre accommodation. €5 one way, €9 return. Departs Cork airport daily every 30mins from 08.00–22.00.

TAXIS There are usually plenty of taxis waiting outside the terminal.

🚗 CAR HIRE

If you plan on hiring a car in Ireland you should check with your travel agent or tour operator if the car-hire company will rent to you if you are under 25 or over 70 years of age. The minimum driving age is 17. You will also need a valid driving licence from your own country free from endorsements. An international driving licence is not acceptable. It is advisable to book the car well in advance during the high season. (See *Getting there and away* in *Chapter 2*, pages 45–7, for further driving information.)

All the following have been approved by the Car Rental Council of Ireland (*www.carrentalcouncil.ie*). Check their websites for special offers.

Alamo/National Car Rental ➘ (airport) 021 431 8623, (city centre) 021 432 0755; e reservations@carhire.ie; www.carhire.ie

Avis ➘ (airport) 021 432 7460, (central reservations) 1890 405 060; www.avis.ie

Budget ➘ (airport) 021 431 4000; e reservations@budget.ie; www.budget.ie

Dan Dooley ➘ (airport) 021 432 1099; www.dan-dooley.ie

Europcar ➘ (airport) 021 491 7300; e info@europcar.ie; www.europcar.ie

Great Island Car Rentals 47 MacCurtain St; ➘ 021 450 3536; e info@greatislandcarrentals; www.greatislandcarrentals.com. This local company offer cars from €35 a day.

Hertz ➘ (airport) 021 496 5849; www.hertz.ie

Sixt/Irish Car Rentals ➘ (airport) 021 431 8644; www.irishcarrentals.com

Thrifty Car Rental ➘ (airport) 021 497 7884; e rent@thrifty.ie; www.thrifty.ie

P PARKING

There are several multi-storey car parks in the city centre, each charging approximately € 1.80 per hour. There are usually discounts if you are staying for a longer period of time. Fines for not collecting your car before closing time are substantial. There is no overnight parking in any of these car parks.

North Main Street Car Park Access from Kyrl's Quay [E2] *Open Mon–Wed 08.30–18.30, Thu & Fri 08.30–21.30, Sat 08.30–18.30, closed Sun.*
Paul Street Car Park Access from Lavitt's Quay [F2] *Open Mon–Sat 07.30 to midnight, Sun 11.30–18.30.*
Roches Stores Car Park Access from Parnell Place [H2] *Open Mon–Sat 08.30–18.30, Thu & Fri 08.30–21.00, closed Sun.*
Carroll's Quay Car Park Access from Carroll's Quay [F2] *Open Mon–Sat 07.00–midnight.*
City Hall Car Park Access from Eglinton Street [J3] *Open Mon–Sat 07.00–21.00.*

Otherwise a parking-disc system is in operation. The paper discs are € 1.80 each and may be purchased from participating shops (most newsagents) and must be scratched to reveal the year, month, day, hour and minute of parking. One disc gives either one or two hours of parking depending on what zone you are in. Check the information plate on the relevant street sign.

🚲 BIKE HIRE

Booking in advance is recommended, especially in July and August.

Cycle Scene 396 Blarney St; ☎ 021 430 1183; e cyclescene@gmail.com; www.cyclescene.ie [E2] Bikes €15–20 per day, €80 per week. Pick-up service available for cycle tours that are in one direction only. *Open Mon–Fri 08.30–17.45, Sat 08.30–17.30.*

Rothar Cycles 55 Barrack St; ☎ 021 431 3133; e info@rotharcycletours.com; www.rotharcycletours.com [E4] Bikes €20 per day, €80 per week, €30 one-way rental service. *Open Mon–Sat 10.00–18.00.*

5 Accommodation

There is no shortage of places to stay in Cork, regardless of budget or transport restrictions. There are places close to the airport, train and bus stations; there are places in the city centre; there are places set in woodland just beyond the city centre. They are all easily accessible, even if you do not have your own set of wheels. Hotel leisure centres are on the increase, with more and more hotels boasting their own swimming pools and holistic treatments. Guesthouses with jacuzzis are not unusual. There are a few reasonable self-catering options and there are several hostels to choose from. You can make reservations with any of the places I have listed either by contacting them directly or by contacting the tourist office (see below). All the accommodation listed in this city guide has been approved by the Irish Tourist Board (Bord Fáilte) and all the hostels are members of Independent Holiday Hostels Ireland (IHH).

Cork City Tourist Office Grand Parade; ℁ 021 425 5100; e corkkerryinfo@failteireland.ie; www.ireland.travel.ie or www.corkkerry.ie. *Open Mon–Fri 09.15–17.15, Sat 09.30–16.30.*
Gulliver Ireland Irish Tourist Board-approved online accommodation reservation service. Free phone ℁ 0800 3698 7414 (Ireland); ℁ 0800 783 8359 (UK); ℁ 1 888 827 3028 (USA); www.gulliverireland.com

71

HOTELS

I have divided the hotels into airport, city centre, outskirts of the city centre (south) and outskirts of the city centre (east). Within those categories, the most expensive or luxurious is first (the two are not to be equated, however; Cork is full of expensive hotels that are not luxurious) followed by the others in descending order. Please refer to the hotel directly for the latest prices. Some hotels offer discounts for booking online. Midweek rates are usually cheaper than weekend rates. See price codes inside front cover. They refer to a standard double room (except in the case of hostel dorms, where the code refers to the rate for one person, and self-catering, where it refers to the apartment rate per night) during high season and include breakfast. Accommodation should be booked well in advance if you're planning on coming over for St Patrick's Day or the Guinness Jazz Festival or other such peak times.

AIRPORT

🏠 **Great Southern Hotel** (81 rooms, 27 smoking) Cork Airport; ☎ 021 494 7500; e res@corkairport-gsh.com; www.gshotels.com

Located within walking distance of the airport, the Great Southern is a handy option for just-arrived/just-about-to-leave stays & is only a 15min drive from the city. Contemporary design, multi-lingual staff, screens in the foyer displaying flight information, reasonably soundproof rooms, a wide range of function rooms & a leisure centre. $$$$ but offers good weekend specials & discounts for booking online. Closed 24–26 Dec.

🏠 **Forte Travelodge** [40 rooms] Blackash, Kinsale Rd Roundabout, Frankfield Rd; ☎ 021 431 0722; www.travelodge.ie

Also convenient for the airport & just a couple of miles from the city centre as well as being on the direct route to west Cork, the Travelodge provides passable accommodation at reasonable prices. Each room can sleep at least 3 adults & a child or 2 adults & 2 children. Smoking rooms available. $$. *Best rates are online. Open all year.*

CITY CENTRE

🏠 **Hayfield Manor Hotel** (88 rooms) Perrott Av, College Rd; ☎ 021 484 5900; e enquiries@hayfieldmanor.ie; www.hayfieldmanor.ie [B4]

Member of Small Luxury Hotels of the World. I think this is where most Corkonians would like to stay if they had the choice. The truly elegant, secluded Hayfield Manor is located in a quiet area but is still within walking distance of the main shopping streets. Entering this multi-award-winning 5-star hotel is like visiting a different world. Antique furniture, beautiful spacious bedrooms, friendly & obliging staff, marble bathrooms, an award-winning restaurant & a private leisure centre where you can be pampered with various massages & treatments, may mean that you never leave this deluxe hotel at all. $$$$$ *(dbl rooms from €250). Open all year.*

🏠 **Kingsley Hotel** (110 rooms) Victoria Cross; ☎ 021 480 0500; e resv@kingsleyhotel.com; www.kingsleyhotel.com [A4]

A very fine hotel situated about 30mins' walk from the city centre. Both elegant & cosy with an open fire in the lounge, the Kingsley does grandeur very well. A good restaurant popular with guests & locals alike, an Ayurvedic spa, a kinesis studio, an outdoor hot tub overlooking the river & a library for pre-dinner drinks;

there's nothing missing really. The rooms come equipped with golf umbrellas, detail being another Kingsley speciality. At the time of writing there was an extension being built & although the Kinglsey is quite a new hotel, there are already 'old' & 'new' rooms. The new rooms are more tastefully decorated, have a separate writing area & the bathrooms are bigger with more of a designer feel, but these are mostly at the front while the old rooms are at the back with the fabulous views of the river & Sunday's Well. No smoking rooms. $$$$$. *Open all year.*

⌂ **Clarion Hotel** (191 Rooms) Lapp's Quay; ☎ 021 422 4900; e info@clarionhotelcorkcity.com; www.clarionhotelcorkcity.com [J2]
One of Cork's newest hotels, the 4-star Clarion is wonderfully modern & calm with a great feeling of space & friendly, courteous staff who seem slightly less jaded than those in some other establishments. Soothingly decorated, air-conditioned rooms; the corner rooms overlook the river & are filled with light. Try & snag one of these if you can (as opposed to a room overlooking the atrium – it's a nice atrium, but …). They have a well-equipped leisure centre, a separate but adjoining conference centre, & a health & beauty spa featuring such delights as hydrotherapy bath treatments as well as others aimed specifically at men. The bar serves Thai food while the restaurant serves modern European cuisine. Smoking rooms subject to availability. Resident pianist in the atrium sounding out instrumental versions of the more sedate chart hits. $$$$$. *Closed 24–26 Dec.*

⌂ **Imperial Hotel** (85 rooms) South Mall; ☎ 021 427 4040; e reservations@imperialhotelcork.ie; www.flynnhotels.com [G3]
A uniformed doorman reflects this hotel's dedication to old-world charm & luxury but it is also discreetly contemporary. Designed by Sir Thomas Deane nearly 200 years ago, both Charles Dickens & William Thackeray

stayed here, as well as Michael Collins who spent his last night here. As well as a restaurant & popular bar, the Imperial also has a very busy French-style brasserie. Their salon & spa includes an Evian hydrotherapy pool. Superbly located in the city centre, the South Mall is busy during the day but quiet at night. This is a good place to stay if you are going for the more expensive rooms; their standard room rate would perhaps be better spent elsewhere. $$$$$. *Closed 24–27 Dec.*

🏠 **Jury's Cork Hotel** [182 rooms] Western Rd; ☎ 021 425 2700; e cork@jurysdoyle.com; www.jurysdoyle.com/cork [D3]
Member of Jury's Doyle Hotel Group. This 4-star hotel re-opened in 2006 following a complete overhaul & its new modern façade – glass elevator included – is much more easy on the eye. Very contemporary with a stylish restaurant & bar overlooking the river, this is a good option for the corporate guest. There are a range of conference rooms (but no proper function room as of yet), the rooms have Pillow Top mattresses, & the leisure centre includes a gym, sauna & steam room, jacuzzi & an 18m pool which also comes with a swimsuit water-extractor. Convenient to the city centre. Smoking rooms available. $$$$$. *Closed Dec 25–26.*

🏠 **Best Western Ambassador Hotel** (60 rooms) Military Hill, St Luke's; ☎ 021 455 1996; e info@ambassadorhotel.ie; www.ambassadorhotel.ie [K1] *No 8 bus from St Patrick's St*
Member of Best Western Hotels. A mere 15min walk from the city centre (but atop a steep hill; might want to bear that in mind), the Ambassador commands spectacular views of the city & harbour from its vantage point on Military Hill. Try to get a south-facing room; they have the balconies, they have the views. A stately red-brick building with an imposing façade (it was once a military hospital), it is not the most luxurious of hotels but it

does have 60 spacious rooms (smoking rooms available), as well as an award-winning restaurant & bar, replete with resident pianist, & a health centre with gym, jacuzzi, steam room & sauna. $$$$. *Closed 24–26 Dec.*

⌂ **Gresham Metropole** (113 rooms) MacCurtain St; ☎ 021 450 8122; e info@gresham-metropolehotel.com; www.gresham-hotels.com [H2]
Refurbished in recent years, this 3-star hotel has spacious rooms, a leisure centre & 25m pool as well as a lively bar. It is also a key live music venue during the Guinness Jazz Festival (see pages 35–6) in October; if you are not a jazz fan, don't even think about staying here during the festival. And even if you are, it might not be the best place to stay if you are after a restful weekend. At other times of year, try to get a room overlooking the river as MacCurtain St is very busy. Smoking rooms available. Walking distance to bus & train stations as well as main shopping area. $$$$. *Open all year.*

⌂ **Jury's Inn** (133 rooms) Anderson's Quay; ☎ 021 494 3000; f 021 427 6144; www.juryinns.com [J2]
Centrally located practical option. Slightly clinical, functional accommodation. Limited car parking. Room-only rates as well as B&B. Smoking rooms available. Check the website for special offers. $$$$. *Closed 23–27 Dec.*

⌂ **Quality Hotel & Leisure Centre** (100 rooms) John Redmond St; ☎ 021 490 8278; e qualshan@indigo.ie; www.choicehotelsireland.ie [F1]
Member of Choice Hotels Ireland. Located close to the Shandon Bells (see pages 176–7) & the historic Butter Exchange (see pages 171–2), the Quality Hotel is also close to the shops & the Opera House. Refurbished in recent times, it is a contemporary hotel with its own pool. Two designated smoking rooms. Room-only rates as well as B&B. I would probably skip the b/fast & go somewhere nice in town. $$$. *Closed 24–27 Dec.*

🏠 **Hotel Isaac's** (36 rooms) 48 MacCurtain St; ✆ 021 450 0011; e cork@isaacs.ie; www.isaacs.ie [H2]
Conveniently located, well-established hotel. A Victorian building with wooden floorboards, a floodlit waterfall & a small courtyard; you can almost forget you're in an urban setting. Because the building is so old, there has been no standardisation of the shape of the rooms. The décor is a little dated & some of the bathrooms are a tad poky & in need of modernisation. The rooms are spread over three floors, the third floor being the smoking floor. Try to get a room at the back of the hotel as MacCurtain St can be quite noisy. The hotel's Greene's Restaurant (see pages 96–7) is located next to the courtyard & is very popular with locals & guests alike. I recommend it. Be sure to make a reservation if you want to eat there. Close to bus & train stations. They tend not to take group bookings. $$$. Weekend specials. Closed 24–27 Dec.

🏠 **Victoria Hotel** (30 rooms) Patrick St/Cook St; ✆ 021 427 8788; e info@thevictoriahotel.com; www.thevictoriahotel.com [G3]
Member of Minotel Hotel Group. Charles Stuart Parnell stayed here, as did James Joyce who later fictionalised his visit in *A Portrait of the Artist as a Young Man*. This compact friendly hotel is bang in the middle of the city & is a handy budget option. Fairly basic, it's not what you want if you're looking for a romantic or peaceful weekend away; its beauty is in its central location. Ideal for those on foot. Smoking permitted in most of the rooms. $$. Closed 24–26 Dec.

OUTSKIRTS OF THE CITY (SOUTH)
🏠 **Maryborough House Hotel** (63 rooms) Maryborough Hill, Douglas; ✆ 021 436 5555; e info@maryborough.ie; www.maryborough.com. For information & reservations within the USA & Canada, contact Lisa Adams; ✆ 1519 751 3290; f 1519 751 0157; e ladams@rogers.com

Only 10mins from the city centre, this delightful 18th-century 4-star hotel is set in 24 acres of gardens & woodland. The foyer sets the tone perfectly — wooden floorboards, candles & a complimentary cocktail on checking in. The owner is very keen on antique furniture & this passion shows. Old meets new in the main house with wonderfully rustic suites featuring gas fireplaces, exposed beams & broadband. Many of the standard rooms have their own balconies overlooking the gardens or, if they are on the ground floor, outdoor decking with garden furniture. In their new extension they also have wonderfully modern & Zen-like basement spa rooms with their own jacuzzis. Both restaurant & bar are stylish, comfortable & buzzy. Staff are professional & friendly. If I had to recommend one out-of-town hotel, this would be it. Smoking rooms available. $$$$$. *Closed 24–26 Dec.*

🏠 **Rochestown Park Hotel** (163 rooms) Rochestown Rd, Douglas; ☎ 021 489 0800;
e res@rochestownpark.com; www.rochestownpark.com
Located in a mature garden setting, this 4-star manor-style hotel is a reliable option for anyone who wants to get away from that hectic city buzz. They have an award-winning leisure centre which includes thalassotherapy (revolves around seawater & seaweed). Close to Mahon Golf Club. The colour schemes vary from floor to floor but are consistently loud; results in a slightly less than contemporary feel. Smoking rooms available. $$$$.
Closed 24–26 Dec.

OUTSKIRTS OF THE CITY (EAST)

🏠 **Ballymaloe House** (33 rooms plus apts) Shanagarry; ☎ 021 465 2531; e res@ballymaloe.ie;
www.ballymaloe.ie
Family-run guesthouse set on a 400-acre farm. Staying at the elegant Ballymaloe is a holiday in itself. This is romantic-weekend-away accommodation. Tastefully decorated rooms, beautiful gardens, delicious food (see pages

117–18), it is very much a country house, rather than an anonymous hotel. They also have self-catering farm apts. Roughly 30km from Cork city, it's only 5km from the coast & ideally placed for scenic constitutionals. Outdoor swimming, golf, tennis & croquet are all possible within the grounds & there is even a play area for children. $$$$$ (standard double room € 250). *They have an interesting range of special offers which are worth looking into. Closed 24–26 Dec.*

🏠 **Sheraton Fota Island Golf Resort & Spa** (131 rooms) Fota Island; ⟍ 021 467 3000; f 021 467 3456; www.sheraton.com

A recent addition to the hotel scene, the 5-star Sheraton is just north of Cobh, itself worth visiting (see pages 195–9), & if you have a car this hotel is a useful base for exploring both Cork city & its surrounds. The exterior is a little off-putting, it's a bit industrial-looking, but this is not a reflection of what lies within. Obviously great for golfers, but with 18 treatment rooms in their spa, it's good for those who like to pamper themselves too. Rooms are spacious & bathrooms feature rather magnificent rainforest showers. If booking online bear in the mind that the dates are in the American format of month/day/year. Smoking rooms available. $$$$$. *Open all year.*

🏠 **Silver Springs Moran Hotel** (109 rooms) Tivoli; ⟍ 021 450 7533; e silversprings@moranhotels.com; www.silverspringshotel.ie

Member of Moran Hotel Group. A large hotel with over 100 rooms, including 5 luxury suites. It is in a rather odd location for Cork: not the city centre but not the rural outskirts either. Just a few mins' drive from the centre, it is not the most convenient option if you are on foot. Handy for those travelling by car from the Rosslare ferry, & it has free parking. They have a leisure & beauty centre, including a 25m swimming pool & indoor tennis. Smoking in most rooms. $$$$. *Closed 25–26 Dec.*

🏠 **Vienna Woods Hotel** (50 rooms) Glanmire; ☎ 021 482 1146; ℮ info@viennawoodshotel.com; www.viennawoodshotel.com

Roughly 10mins' drive from the city centre, this comfortable country-house hotel is set in 20 acres of woodland, which you can either see as isolated or secluded, depending on your mindset. Convenient for Cobh & Fota & for anyone coming from Rosslare. Smoking rooms available. $$$$. *Closed 24–26 Dec.*

🏠 **Hotel Ibis** (100 rooms) Lee Tunnel Roundabout, Dunkettle; ☎ 021 435 4354; f 021 435 4202; www.ibishotel.com

A good budget option if you have your own car & don't want to stay in the city centre. Taxis to the city centre €10–15. Useful if arriving from Rosslare or Dublin. A fairly standard Ibis with rooms slightly larger than average. Smoking rooms available. $$. *Open all year.*

GUESTHOUSES

There are dozens of high-quality guesthouses all along Western Road. If you are looking for something a little cheaper, there are quite a few reasonable options on the Lower Glanmire Road near the train station. Bed and breakfast rates include breakfast and are per person sharing per night. It is worth bearing in mind that a reasonably priced bed and breakfast is sometimes nicer than a more expensive hotel.

🏠 **Paradiso Rooms** (3 rooms) 16 Lancaster Quay (directly above Café Paradiso); ☎ 021 427 7939; ℮ info@cafeparadiso.ie; www.cafeparadiso.ie [D3]

Centrally located townhouse accommodation opened in September 2005 by those who run the restaurant (see pages 92–3), there are just 3 rooms, aimed at those who want to enjoy the 'complete Paradiso experience'. Each room has its own ambience but all are decorated in a very personal style that is both contemporary & arty. Vegetarian b/fast included in the rate: one of the best breakfasts in the city. $$$$$. *Closed Sun & Mon.*

🏠 **Lancaster Lodge** (48 rooms) Lancaster Quay, Western Rd; 📞 021 425 1125; e info@lancasterlodge.com; www.lancasterlodge.com [D3]
Located back from the busy Western Road (the River Lee lies between the Lodge & the road) the front of the guesthouse has been soundproofed so the noise is not an issue. Very handy location, catering mostly for corporate guests; free parking, award-winning breakfasts, spacious rooms with subtle contemporary design. Jacuzzi suites have very comfortable Pillow Top beds. The rooms at the back all have terrific views of St Finbarre's Cathedral. Friendly & efficient staff. The building is entirely non-smoking. A good central option. $$$$. *Closed Dec 24–29.*

🏠 **Garnish House** (14 rooms) Western Rd; 📞 021 4275111; e info@garnish.ie; www.garnish.ie [B3]
Located opposite the main gates of University College Cork (UCC), this is another luxury B&B with jacuzzis featuring in some of the rooms. This place is renowned for the wonderful welcome it extends to all its guests, with tea & scones provided to help you settle in. The b/fast menu is also very impressive with 30 gourmet options to choose from: try the porridge with Jameson whiskey. $$$. *Open all year.*

🏠 **Crawford Guesthouse** (12 rooms) Western Rd; 📞 021 427 9000; e info@crawfordguesthouse.com; www.crawfordguesthouse.com [B3]
Located directly across from UCC, halfway between the main entrance & the Gaol Cross entrance, this top-class

B&B offers luxury en suites, some of which come with jacuzzis. All the rooms are beautifully furnished & a good night's sleep is guaranteed with the orthopaedic 6ft king-size beds although if you are in a room at the front of the house, the traffic may disturb your sleep, as Western Road is very busy. $$$. *Closed 23 Dec–2 Jan.*

🏠 **Acorn House** (9 rooms) 14 St Patrick's Hill; ✆/f 021 450 2474; e info@acornhouse-cork.com; www.acornhouse-cork.com [G1]
Nearly 200 years old, this Georgian house has been nicely refurbished with each room pleasantly decorated. Very hospitable with a decent Irish b/fast that should set you up for the day. It is located on a very steep hill, so bear this in mind when booking. City-centre location & just a 5min walk to the bus & train stations. $$$. *Closed 22 Dec–16 Jan.*

🏠 **Auburn House** (8 rooms, plus 3 rooms across road) Garfield Terr, Wellington Rd; ✆ 021 450 8555; e info@auburnguesthouse.com; www.auburnguesthouse.com [J1]
Located on the north side of the river, this guesthouse is within easy walking distance of the city centre & is also very close to both the train & bus stations. Parking available for those with cars. Not all rooms are en suite & this is reflected in the price. The building is entirely non-smoking. Vegetarian breakfasts available. $$. *Closed over Christmas.*

HOSTELS

All the hostels are ITB approved. No membership is required and all ages are welcome. All hostels are walking distance from the city centre. Rates at some hostels vary a little depending on the season and/or the time of the week. Dorm beds are on average € 16 each. All the hostels also offer good value twins and/or doubles.

🏠 **Brú Bar & Hostel** (sleeps 93) 57 MacCurtain St; ☎ 021 455 9667; e info@bruhostel.com; www.bruhostel.com [H2]
Voted 7th-best hostel in the world by *Hostel World* (*www.hostelworld.com*). Over 90 beds, all rooms en suite. No smoking rooms. Helpful & knowledgeable staff. Free internet access, laundry facilities, fully equipped kitchen, TV room, 24hr access, towel hire, bicycle & luggage storage, free b/fast. Fully licensed resident's bar open till 4.00 (popular with locals too). Private rooms (sleep 3, double & single), 6-bed dorms, 4-bed dorms, mixed or all-female. Same rates all year round. *Dorms $; private rooms $$. Closed 24–25 Dec.*

🏠 **Cork International Youth Hostel** (sleeps 98) 1–2 Redclyffe, Western Rd; ☎ 021 454 3289; e mailbox@anoige.ie; www.irelandyha.org [B3] *No 8 bus from Patrick St*
Located opposite UCC, near Gaol Cross. Open 24hrs. Single-sex dorms only. En-suite bedrooms & dorms. Large self-catering kitchen. TV/video room. Luggage storage. Bed linen. French- & Polish-speaking staff. Supplement of € 2 for Fri & Sat night stays, bank holiday & special-event weekends. B/fast is extra. Discounts for members of An Óige (Hostelling International). *Dorms $; doubles $$. Closed over Christmas.*

🏠 **Kinlay House** (41 rooms) Bob & Joan's Walk, Shandon; ☎ 021 450 8966; e info@kinlayhousecork.ie; www.kinlayhouse.ie [F1]
Part of a chain, Kinlay House also have hostels in Dublin & Galway. Member of IHH (Independent Holiday Hostels; *www.hostels-ireland.com*). Clean & spacious, facilities include free Continental b/fast before 09.30, bed

linen, self-catering kitchen & barbecue area. No curfew, 24hr staffing, bureau de change, bicycle storage, security lockers/luggage storage, tourist information & booking service, free car parking, internet access, international pay phones, TV lounge, laundry service. Guests are entitled to discounts at a nearby health & fitness club. Close to bus & train stations. Twin privates, 8-bed mixed dorms en suite, 10-bed female dorms en suite. *Dorms* $; *twins* $$. *Open all year.*

⌂ **Sheila's Budget Accommodation Centre** (43 rooms) 3 Belgrave Pl, Wellington Rd; ✆ 021 450 5562; e info@sheilashostel.ie; www.sheilashostel.ie [J1]
Member of IHH. Facilities include free hot showers, sauna, internet access, TV/video room, well-equipped self-catering kitchen, large dining room, common room, secure luggage storage, safety deposit boxes, cinema room, convenience store, foreign exchange, bicycle & car hire, tourist information. Rooms are small but colourful & clean. No curfew, no lock-out, 24-hour CCTV security, key card access. B/fast is extra. Just a 5min walk from the bus & train stations. Twin privates, 8-bed mixed dorms en suite, 10-bed female dorm en suite. *Dorms* $; *twins* $$. *Closed 24–25 Dec.*

SELF-CATERING

The following are ITB approved.

⌂ **DeansHall Self-Catering Accommodation** (54 apts) Crosses Green; ✆ 021 431 2623; e info@deanshall.com (enquiries), bookings@deanshall.com (bookings); www.deanshall.com [E3]
Normally let out to students during the college year, DeansHall also caters for holidaymakers in the summer

vacation, with 3-bedroom apts (up to 4 people) & 5-bedroom apts (up to 6 people). Group rates available. Kitchens are fully equipped & each apartment has a direct-dial telephone. The reception desk is open Mon–Fri, 08.00–19.00. DeansHall is centrally located but is in a quiet area close to St Finbarre's Cathedral (see pages 177–8). Proby's Bistro (see pages 105–6) is next door. *3-bedroom apts $$$$; 5-bedroom apts $$$$$. Open 14 Jun–30 Aug.*

🏠 **Isaac's Apartments** (11 apts) 48 MacCurtain St; ☏ 021 450 0011; e cork@isaacs.ie; www.isaacs.ie [H2] Isaac's has 2-bedroom apts (up to 4 people) & 3-bedroom apts (up to 6 people). Weekend & weekly rates are also available. These rates may not apply, however, for special-event or bank holiday weekends. Greene's Restaurant (see *Chapter 6*, pages 96–7) is downstairs, the kitchens are fully equipped, & the apts are close to the main shopping area as well as the bus & train stations. *2-bedroom apts $$$$– $$$$$ (depending on the season); 3-bedroom apts $$$$$. Open all year.*

6 Eating and Drinking

There was a time when the most exotic fare in Cork was Italian, and even then the menu was unlikely to stretch much beyond spaghetti bolognese and lasagne (and never the vegetarian kind, before you ask). Home cooking was not much more adventurous; to this day in Ireland there are mothers who will not stray from the tried and tested meat-and-two-veg format, potatoes of course being a staple (then again, there are few sons arguing with this winning formula). Luckily things have changed. There are plenty of restaurants to choose from, lots of different ethnicities and vegetarians no longer have to content themselves with a spur-of-the-moment vegetarian lasagne rustled up by an unimaginative chef.

There are eateries to cater for every budget. Whether you're watching the pennies or looking to splurge, you can eat well for your money. Quite a few places offer Early Bird menus (ordering early in the evening for a reduced-price meal from a set menu), while others offer fixed-price lunch menus which often include a complimentary glass of wine. If you are trying to stretch your money, it is a good idea to avail yourself of one of these lunch menus later in the afternoon as a substitute for a main meal in the evening as they offer greater value for money and can be very filling. Many restaurants also offer a take-away option.

These days the emphasis is all on locally sourced free-range and organic produce. Fresh fish and seafood form a large component of most menus and creative vegetarian dishes are widely available. Many restaurants now rely on small artisan producers to supply high-quality ingredients – cheese, fruit and vegetables, meat and fish, eggs – so you can be assured that you are getting value for money as well as contributing to the local economy. There is perhaps an over-reliance on Bailey's – Bailey's cheesecake, Bailey's porridge, Bailey's coffee – and whiskey; there's a lot of this around, although to be honest, hotel restaurants tend to be the main culprits.

If you are invited into someone's home, you may get to try some of the local specialities, namely tripe and *drisheen* (see box, pages 98–9) or even the lesser-known skirts and kidneys. It has to be said that if it is not the home of a born-and-bred local, you are unlikely to be presented with the aforementioned delicacies. Another local touch in the majority of Cork restaurants and cafés is that the black tea on offer is invariably the locally blended Barry's Tea and the menus often say as much. Remember that it is illegal to smoke in restaurants and cafés (see *Chapter 2*, box, page 51). Many restaurants are closed on Sundays.

RESTAURANTS

The bulk of Cork's restaurants fall into the mid-range category, many of them providing a wide range of prices within their menus, thus excluding no-one really. Many of them have various deals on offer at different times of the day. I've listed all the restaurants alphabetically rather than try to group them together under different categories. This is not an exhaustive list; it includes my recommendations only, and where there are a few restaurants serving similar cuisine, I've recommended the one I think is the best. If you want to just wander around and find someplace for yourself, there are a lot of different restaurants centred around Princes Street and Cook Street, between Oliver Plunkett Street and South Mall.

✕ **The Ambassador** 3 Cook St; ✆ 021 427 3261/427 1026; www.ambassadorrestaurant.ie [G3]
Popular well-established Chinese restaurant. Plenty of choice, from seafood (steamed scallops with garlic & black bean sauce) to poultry (chicken in orange sauce), from chop suey to curries to sweet & sour, & of course grilled black pepper sirloin steaks for those who always pick steak. *Above average; mains* **$$$$**. *Open daily 17.30–midnight.*

✕ **Amicus** 14a French Church St; ✆ 021 427 6455 [F2]
Situated in the heart of Cork's Huguenot Quarter, Amicus is a small but busy restaurant usually packed to capacity at all hours of the day. At the time of writing Amicus was still at this address but was preparing to relocate to the former Gingerbread House premises just around the corner on Rory Gallagher Square. They were planning to retain the French Church St premises for their new restaurant, Nutmeg, but no further details were available. The new premises are much larger which is just what Amicus needs as it seems to be constantly full. Small wonder with a b/fast, day & evening menu offering the best in contemporary European cuisine 7 days a week. Simple modern décor, softly lit tables, good music, lively conversation, Amicus seems to have a life of its own set apart from the shopping bustle on the street. On milder days you can sit outside &

bask in the warmth of the on-hand heaters whilst sipping your cappuccino & watching all human life swarm past. The day menu includes soups, salads, gourmet sandwich plates, a host of pasta dishes & several main courses all for a very reasonable price. Portions are generous & very filling. The evening menu is like an expanded, slightly more expensive version of the day menu, & includes a selection of starters as well as a range of seafood dishes. Portions are just as generous, & there are plenty of vegetarian options. A typical main course might be breast of chicken filled with pistachio & raisin stuffing, served with a whiskey cream, sautéed greens & chive mash. Tasty food, & a great ambience. *Mid-range; mains* $$$. *Open Mon–Sat 10.00–22.30, Sun 12.00–21.00.*

✖ Banna Thai 15 Maylor St; ☎ 021 425 1571; www.bannathairestaurant.com [G2]

Commitment issues prevent me from declaring this restaurant my favourite in Cork, or at any rate my favourite Thai restaurant, but whenever I'm asked where I would like to go for dinner, Banna Thai is a frequent response. I should warn you that I like my food hot (I keep a jar of cayenne pepper in my locker at work) & if you want a meal that will blow your head off then this is the place for you. But don't let that put you off. Thai food is not just about the fiery spikiness of the chillies. It is fragrant, fresh food, cleansing even, full of mellow flavours but with bite. Earthy coriander, warming ginger, lemongrass, coconut milk – these are light refreshing ingredients which combine to make the most flavoursome of dishes, & flavoursome dishes is what Banna Thai is all about. Situated on Maylor St between Brown Thomas & Roches stores, it is an airy, modern restaurant, tastefully decorated with a few typically Thai furnishings. There is a set lunch special which includes a starter (7 to choose from), main course (14 options, each served with boiled rice or egg rice) & tea or coffee. The dinner menu is extensive with over 50 dishes on offer including starters, soups, mains & side dishes. Mains vary from simple stir-fried dishes to their house specials, for example Yum Nau, a Thai-beef warm salad with char-grilled strips of lean beef mixed with lemongrass, onions, kaffir lime leaves, coriander & tossed with a tangy Thai dressing. They also do special set-menus for private functions. Gaeng Panang, their Panang curry, is one of my favourite dishes. Choose from beef, pork, prawns, chicken or veg for this wonderfully spicy curry flavoured with coconut milk & a variety of traditional Thai herbs — absolutely divine. Complimentary Thai prawn crackers materialise on the table moments after you sit down & everyone is given the option of having their food either hot or spicy. Choose carefully & don't overestimate your heat threshold. Hot is hot as all hell & will have you shedding tears & clothes at an indecent rate. If you are on the move, you'll be glad to hear they also do take-away (10% discount). *Mid-range; mains $$$. Open Mon–Thu 12.00–15.30, 17.30–22.00, Fri & Sat 12.00–23.00, Sun 13.00–22.00.*

✗ **Bombay Palace** 14–15 Cook St; ☎ 021 427 3366 [G3]
One of the better Indian restaurants in town, its décor has an edge over the others by not being too cluttered or dark & by suffusing everything in a warm roseate glow. The menu is extensive & typical; the food is cooked to perfection; the wine selection is passable (they also have Indian beers on offer); the prices are reasonable; there are plenty of vegetarian dishes; the service is friendly & unobtrusive & they provide a take-away service. *Mid-range; mains $$$. Open for lunch Tue–Sat 12.30–14.30, dinner Mon–Sun 17.30–23.30.*

✗ **Boqueria** 6 Bridge St; ☎ 021 455 9049; e tapas@boqueriasixbridgest.com [G2]
Once an old man's pub, now an atmospheric tapas bar. Spain meets Ireland with a large selection of Spanish nibbles forged from the finest produce Cork has to offer — Arbutus bread, Hegarty's cheddar, Ardsallagh goat's cheese, all those artisan foodstuffs that tempt you in the English Market. Here they are in their Spanish incarnation, for example piquillos: sweet roasted red peppers stuffed with Ardsallagh goat's cheese & crushed

almonds. This is a great place to come with a gang of friends so you can all order lots of different things & everyone gets to try a bit of everything. Yummy food, & terrific wines to accompany it. Great at any time of day. All the food is freshly prepared. *Mid-range; tapas* $$. *Open Mon–Sat 09.00–23.00, Sun 16.00–22.00.*

✗ **Café Mexicana** Carey's Lane; ☎ 021 427 6433; www.cafemexicana.net [F2]
The first Mexican restaurant in Ireland, Café Mexicana has been providing the denizens of Cork city with the most incredibly moreish food since 1990. Hidden down a narrow little lane in the city centre, its Mexican music seeping onto the street quickly points the way. As well as several Mayan artefacts, the window also displays a certificate from the Mayan tourist board declaring Café Mexicana an official promoter of Mexico in Ireland. Certainly once you walk through the door you could forget you are in cold damp Cork; a vibrant, festive, intimate candlelit atmosphere awaits within. Then there's the food. Quesadillas, enchiladas, tacos, fajitas, burritos, nachos, sour cream, salsa, guacamole, chillies, refried beans & of course tequila. This is their extensive menu simplified in the extreme. Here there's something for everyone: the vegetarians, the meat-eaters, the seafood fanatics, the dessert divas. Prices vary dramatically too, with something to suit every pocket. I recommend the Nachos Enfrijolados (includes refried beans), creamy & satisfying, & like all of Café Mexicana's meals they're accompanied with sour cream & two gutsy chilli salsas. This is comfort food to warm you up. If desserts are your thing, try their Mexican Grandma's Cake, a chilled gateau of coffee, rum & fresh cream, topped with chocolate, or perhaps their banana & tequila cake. Speaking of which, they also do a mean margarita pitcher. *Mid-range; mains* $$$. *Open daily 12.00–late.*

✗ **Café de la Paix** 16 Washington St West; ☎ 021 427 9556; e info @ cafedelapaixcork.com; www.cafedelapaixcork.com [E3]

A café & wine bar, this is a lovely little place to come in nice weather as they have outdoor decking directly over the river. However it is equally nice when the weather is miserable as it is full of natural light & always feels very bright (but not in a harsh glaring kind of way) & really manages to lift your spirits. I like this place when it's busy; if it's quiet it's the kind of place where you can hear every scrape of every chair, so it's not so good for the self-conscious. Luckily it does tend to be quite busy. For lunch I recommend the Café de la Paix salad — too many delicious components to list here — & the blue cheese & bacon panini is also very good. Mains range from deep-fried risotto balls with chorizo & yoghurt dip to a bruchetta combo plate for which you choose three pretty good toppings; 'toppings' seems not quite a good enough word for them: for example, serrano ham, mozzarella & tapenade, & that's just one topping. The wine list is pretty extensive, so you'll definitely find something to your taste. *Mid-range; mains* $$$. *B/fast 08.00–12.00, lunch 12.00–16.00, dinner 17.00–21.30.*

✕ **Café Paradiso** 16 Lancaster Quay; ✆ 021 427 7939; 📧 info@cafeparadiso.ie; www.cafeparadiso.ie [D3]
One of the best vegetarian restaurants in Ireland, if not the best, this relaxed café/restaurant is a must — even if you are not vegetarian. It's open for b/fast & lunch as well as dinner, though dining here in the evening is pretty much an impossibility without a reservation. Be warned, however, that this is not the place to go if you are absolutely starving & rather indifferent as to what fills the gap. The emphasis here is on quality, not quantity, so buy yourself a veggie burger & come back another day. Founded & run by Denis Cotter, a native of Cork, & Bridget Healy from New Zealand, Café Paradiso has a menu that is both eclectic & mouth-watering, set off by the slightly bohemian décor. The moment you walk through the door you feel as if you've entered a room full of friends, so lively, relaxed & intimate is the atmosphere. Then there's the food — playful & daring — & not a Bailey's-soaked morsel in sight. For starters try beetroot mousse with orange-

scented yoghurt, watercress & fennel crispbreads. I particularly enjoyed the pumpkin & goat's cheese mousse with hazelnut praline, parsley & pumpkin-seed pesto, capers & spiced crsipbread when I was there. Follow it with feta, pistachio & couscous cake with sweet & hot pepper relish, sweet-spiced kale, coriander yoghurt & chickpeas with fresh chilli & tomato or the delicious pan-fried oyster mushrooms in a cider cream with grilled sage & smoked Gubbeen polenta, New Zealand spinach & balsamic-roasted beets. Hum & haw over the dessert menu for a while & then maybe try the anise-baked figs with pistachio baklava & cardamom yoghurt. From then on you'll be including Café Paradiso gift vouchers on your Christmas wish-list. As an accompaniment, they specialise in the wines of New Zealand & Italy; in fact they have a policy of no French wines. If you want to have a go at cooking this kind of food for yourself, Denis has also written two critically acclaimed cookbooks, *The Café Paradiso Cookbook* & *Café Paradiso Seasons* (see Chapter 13, *Further information*, pages 221–2), both available in local & nationwide bookshops as well as in the restaurant itself. They now also have accommodation for those who want to enjoy the 'complete Paradiso experience' (see pages 80–1). Email bookings not accepted. *Expensive; mains* **$$$$$**. *Open Tue–Sat, lunch 12.30–15.00, dinner 18.30–22.30 (last orders). Closed Sun & Mon.*

✗ **Captain America's Cookhouse and Bar** 4–5 South Main St; ✆ 021 427 8972; e cork@captainamericas.com; www.captainamericas.com [E3]
Specialising in hamburgers & cocktails, this is a good family venue. They also have a Rock 'n' Roll Museum with all manner of music memorabilia – a signed White Stripes guitar, Larry Mullen's drumsticks, Debbie Harry's shoes & so on. Sundays are their special 'kids days', when they have clowns & colouring competitions & the like. They also have a good kids menu – everything served with chips, the kids will be happy, & everything's very reasonably priced too. Adults can look forward to a range of burgers & steaks, all made from

100% premium Irish beef, as well as a range of organic dishes & a full bar. *Mid-range; mains* $$$. *Open daily from noon.*

✕ Ristorante Casanova 87 North Main St; ☎ 021 485 1111 [E2]
Bijou Italian restaurant, hip & popular. The lunch menu includes all the usual suspects — pasta dishes, pizzas, burgers & paninis. Dinner options vary in price with popular dishes such as lasagne at the bottom end of the scale & then the more exotic handmade ravioli filled with spinach & ricotta, served with truffles, butter & parmesan quite rightly at the upper end. *Mid-range; mains* $$$. *Lunch 11.30–16.30, dinner 17.00–22.00 midweek, 17.00–22.30 Sat, 18.00–22.00 Sun. Live piano music Thu, Fri and Sat night.*

✕ Castelli's Restaurant 29 Princes St; ☎ 021 427 3888 [G3]
A bit like sitting in someone's kitchen, Castelli's is by no means a posh restaurant. Small & cosy, with lino & wooden booths & a glass ceiling, the atmosphere is almost familial. The staff are very friendly & the food is tasty as well as reasonably priced. The menu is typical — pastas & pizzas, seafood & several meat-oriented dishes. They have a set Early Bird menu of starter, main & tea/coffee. Competitively priced for lunch too. If you're looking for a relaxing but intimate evening & want to gorge yourself on the comfort food that is pasta, Castelli's is a good option. *Mid-range; mains* $$$. *Open daily 12.00–midnight. Early Bird menu 17.00–20.00.*

✕ Curran's Restaurant 5 Adelaide St; ☎ 021 422 3954; www.curranscork.com [E2]
This is a popular down-to-earth restaurant with a roof garden which is fab in summer, especially if you're a smoker. Rustic-looking, the restaurant is built entirely from materials salvaged from Cork's demolished buildings. Numerous artefacts include an elevator, old railings, a staircase & a harp. The food is simple but good. They

do a soup & sandwich special & the choice of sandwiches includes their Tuscan vegetarian melt with mushrooms, peppers, tomatoes & pesto on a toasted bap. Scones in the morning with jam & cream are sweet & comforting. Thai marinated chicken is a typical evening main course. *Mid-range; mains* $$$. *Open Mon–Wed & Sun 09.30–22.00, Thu–Sat 09.30–23.00.*

✕ **Fenn's Quay** 5 Fenn's Quay; ☎ 021 427 9527; www.fennsquay.ie [E3]
A small intimate restaurant which can seat no more than 60 people; I think I probably don't eat in Fenn's Quay often enough. It looks dark from the outside, but during the day if you sit at the front with its whitewashed walls & large window, there's actually a surprising amount of light in there. The background jazz music is a soothing but lively accompaniment to the many delicious dishes on offer here. If you're just looking for something basic you can have soup or house-cut potato chips & garlic mayonnaise for a very reasonable price. The sandwiches are also good, brie & tomato being one example of a typical filling. They also do a lunch deal comprising a soup, sandwich & tea, coffee or a soft drink. If you're looking for something a bit more adventurous try their Clonakilty black pudding with potato pancake & spiced apple. Salads are dressed in the silkiest vinaigrette I've come across in a long time. If you need something with more substance, you can choose from their à la carte lunch menu which includes roast chicken breast wrapped in prosciutto with sage, Parmesan potatoes, green beans & mustard cream. Desserts include their gluten-free house speciality V'ice-cream (sweet Pedro Ximenez sherry with vanilla ice cream) & the very good Icepresso (vanilla ice cream with hot espresso). The latter is perhaps more a beverage than a dessert but it is luscious & anyway, what's in a name? Their dinner menu is of a similar style & quality, for example roast loin of pork with apple & siuchuan pepper relish, red cabbage & mash. *Mid-range; mains* $$$. *Service charge of 10% for groups of 6 or more, 1 bill per table. Open Mon–Sat 10.00–22.00 (last orders). Early Bird menu Mon–Sat, before 19.30. Closed Sun.*

✗ Gino's 7 Winthrop St; ✆ 021 427 4485 [G3]

If you have kids, Gino's is perfect for that pizza & ice-cream hit. Loads of toppings, loads of flavours & a bright, cheery interior. Try the Death by Chocolate. *Mid-range; mains* **$$$**. *Open daily 12.30–22.30.*

✗ Greene's Restaurant 48 MacCurtain St; ✆ 021 455 2279; **e** greenes@isaacs.ie; www.isaacs.ie [H2].
Go through the cobblestone arch next to Isaac's, Greene's Restaurant is at the back on the right.
Particularly lovely in summer when you can sit outside next to the waterfall, Greene's is also inviting in winter with its warm terracotta hues & subtle lighting. Besides, an abundance of windows & glass doors means that the winter diner is not deprived of the waterfall view either. Greene's menu is eclectic & changes regularly – providing you with further excuses to go back there. Seafood features strongly with many of the starters & main courses consisting of fish or shellfish of some kind. Starters include a very interesting *millefeuille* of Clonakilty black pudding & caramelized apples on a sage potato cake with a honey & grain mustard dressing. It's always good to see local specialities reinvented. Main courses are equally imaginative. You can have anything from pan-roasted hake with paprika, chorizo on rosti potatoes, creamy spinach & smoked salmon with rocket, lime & chorizo dressing to pan-seared T-bone steak served with grilled tomatoes, homemade chips & a brandy peppercorn sauce. Vegetarians can go for the selection of wild mushrooms pan-fried in garlic butter on a tart fine of caramelised cherry tomatoes, Ardsallagh goat's cheese, black olive & sunblush tomato tapenade. All the main courses are served with vegetables & potatoes; in other words, you won't be going hungry. Desserts include fruity options, chocolatey options & truly exotic options. Rather unusual is the rolled fresh fruit sushi with lemon coconut milk rice, pistachio Anglaise & a lime dipping sauce. They also have an Irish Farmhouse Cheeseplate if desserts are not your thing. Service is friendly if a little inconsistent – they might take your coat, they might not, & if you feel your pocket can't stretch to the full

dinner menu, there is always the three-course Early Bird menu available daily between 18.00–19.00. *Expensive; mains* $$$$$. Service charge of 10% for groups of 10 or more. Open daily, b/fast 07.00–10.00; lunch Mon–Sat 12.00–17.00, Sun 12.30–16.00; dinner Mon–Thu 18.00–22.00, Fri and Sat 18.00–22.30, Sun 18.00–21.30. Early Bird menu daily 18.00–19.00.

✘ **Il Padrino** 21 Cook St; ✆ 021 427 1544; www.ilpadrinorestaurant.com [G3]
This is a small stylish Italian restaurant where a brief description of some of their tantalising dishes will more than suffice to tempt you through their door – tagliatelle with fresh salmon, garlic, dill weed, thyme & lemon, flamed with brandy & cooked in cream, fresh basil & sundried tomato pesto. Or fettuccine with garlic, broccoli, sundried tomatoes & fresh basil pesto in a pomodoro & cream sauce. I've eaten here several times, with considerable gaps between each visit, & it is always good. Consistency, I like that. Their four-cheese farfalle is excellent & it's served with really good garlic bread. Like any Italian, they do pizzas as well as pastas & all the usual Italian desserts. *Mid-range; mains* $$$. Open Mon–Fri 11.30–late, Sat–Sun 12.00–late.

✘ **Indian Palace** 31 Princes St; ✆ 021 427 3690; e indianpalace@eircom.net [G3]
Dark & atmospheric & perhaps something of a feng shui nightmare with its 'more is more' policy when it comes to tapestries, statues, plants & other random artefacts, the Indian Palace has an ever so slightly run-down feel, compounded by its skipping CD player, but the food is good & reasonably priced. Their menu is extensive & as with many Indian restaurants, if you want something that isn't there, they will try & oblige you. They also specialise in Goanese cuisine & have won awards in the past for their curries. The wine selection is not great, offering neither choice nor value for money, but they do also have Indian beers. Service

TRIPE AND DRISHEEN

Tripe and drisheen are not to everyone's taste. Sheep's stomach and long fat sausages made from dried sheep's blood and herbs may not have you licking your lips in anticipation, but they are Cork specialities and if you fancy yourself as a world food *connoisseur* and are of a strong constitution, then you absolutely must try them. The Farmgate Café upstairs in the English Market (see page 109) serves the dish cooked and ready for consumption but if you fancy cooking it yourself the following is the recipe as supplied by O'Reilly's, the tripe and drisheen stall in the English Market:

INGREDIENTS

1½lb tripe	¼ tsp pepper	2 onions
2 pints water	3oz margarine	1½ pints milk
1 tsp salt	3oz flour	

is friendly, there are complimentary poppadoms & dips & they can usually fit you in without a booking, although it is worth bearing in mind that there is a 10% discount on website bookings. They also have a take-away service. *Mid-range; mains* **$$$**. *Open for dinner Mon–Sat 17.00–midnight, Sun 16.00–midnight. Open for lunch Mon–Sat 12.30–14.30.*

METHOD Cut the tripe in three-inch strips about one inch wide. Place in a saucepan with water, salt and pepper and bring to the boil. Simmer for 40–45 minutes. Drain into a colander and save half a pint of the strained water.

Melt the margarine over a low heat, stir in the flour and chopped onions and cook until it forms a paste. Gradually add the half pint of water stock, some salt and pepper, and the milk and allow the sauce to thicken.

Add the tripe and drisheen (which is already cooked and only needs to be warmed up) and simmer for a further two minutes. Serve with boiled potatoes.

VARIATIONS To lighten or change the flavour of the tripe sauce you can try blending it with a packet of soup before adding the tripe. Celery or leek soup are suggested.

Alternatively you can serve the tripe with milk thickened by cornflour. Boil a pint of milk and just as it comes to the boil add two teaspoons of cornflour that have already been blended with a little cold milk. Cook for two to three minutes and pour over the tripe.

✘ **Isaac's** 48 MacCurtain St; ✆ 021 450 3805; e isaacs@iol.ie [H2]
This is a busy restaurant with a cosmopolitan feel. Located next to Isaac's Hotel it is not actually related to the hotel in any way; Greene's, under the archway, is the hotel restaurant. A diverse & reasonably priced lunch menu includes fried Ardsallagh goat's cheese with roast beetroot, peppers & basil vinaigrette or tempura with tiger prawns, scallions, aubergine, soy dipping sauce, pickled onion & wasabi. Desserts include the rather

sensational chocolate St Émilion with macaroons & brandy. Dinner includes roast stuffed chicken in pancetta with champ, chive sauce & spiced cranberry sauce. The dinner & lunch dessert menus are the same. Their specials change twice-daily, their coffee is organic & fair trade (it's a very nice place to go for coffee during the day) & most of their dishes can be prepared with a little oil & no dairy — just let them know if that's what you want. *Mid-range; mains $$$. 10% service charge on parties of 8 or more & on bank holidays. Open Mon–Sat 10.00–22.30, Sun 18.30–21.00.*

✘ **The Ivory Tower** The Exchange Buildings, 33 Princes St; ☎ 021 427 4665; ivorytower@eircom.net; www.seamusoconnell.com [G3]

Hailed by *The Observer* as 'probably one of the best restaurants in the British Isles', the Ivory Tower is unassuming in aspect & not at all what one would expect from any restaurant with an imposing reputation. Located upstairs on the corner of Princes & Oliver Plunkett streets, a discreetly lit menu is the only indication that there is anything of interest beyond its doors. I often stop to have a look at the menu out of curiosity, but the writing is so cramped together & the font used not so easy on the eye, that I usually give up after the 'Surprise Taster'. What is clear is that for approx €60 you can have a surprise taster, a starter, a soup or sorbet, a main course & a dessert. All produce is organic or wild & you don't have to choose from every course, but it will still cost the same. There is also an 8-course tasting menu for approx €75. When you do go through the doors, the first thing that strikes you is the bohemian element — the battered staircase, the candles, the incense, the paintings, the complete lack of any pretension or even just signs indicating where to go. Up the stairs, past the kitchen & into the kind of dining area you'd like in your own home, where you'll be promptly be sent back downstairs again if you don't have a reservation. At least that's what happened to me the first time I sauntered in on the spur of the moment. So don't be disappointed & DO make a reservation: this place is fab. My surprise taster was asparagus in batter with celeriac & truffle cream. It was only a little thing, but the absolutely divine flavour lingered for ages, which was just as well as the service, while very friendly & informal, was not the fastest. The Ivory Tower is a night out in itself, it's the absolute antithesis to fast food, & is a place to linger (so it might be an idea not to go on a Saturday when there are only two sittings & so less time at the table). For my starter I chose a goat's blue-cheese soufflé in a globe artichoke with vanilla beurre blanche. Sensation-wise it reminded me of candy floss; you cram a load in & it just sort of dissolves into a creamy nothingness — it was dreamy, & it looked great. I followed that up with a cleansing sorbet of guava, tequila, quinine & grapefruit served to me in a shot glass. Tart & icy, it refreshed my palate & prepped it for the flavours to follow. Handmade gnocchi with artichokes, celeriac, salsify & white truffle comprised my main course. I go weak at the knees for gnocchi & this dish did not disappoint. Having cleaned the plate I was well & truly stuffed but couldn't resist their desserts. My companion & I agreed to split a dessert & a cheeseboard. I wanted the strawberry & saffron crème brulée, he wanted the Valrhona chocolate & jasmine silk cake. He won. And it was good, but what was especially yummy was the delicately flavoured liquorice ice cream that accompanied it. I wouldn't have thought it, but it worked. But so many of Seamus O'Connell's dishes are based on just that premise: the yoking together of disparate ingredients to create an unexpectedly divine dish, the loin of venison with chocolate sauce another case in point. This is a small, intimate restaurant, laid-back & slightly haphazard with eclectic but appropriate tunes to boot, & wonderful, if unorthodox food — don't miss it. *Expensive; mains* $$$$$. *Japanese menu (sushi & sashimi with sake & jazz) Tue 18.00–22.00, lunch 12.00–15.00, dinner Wed–Sun from 19.00. Two sittings on Sat, 19.00 & 21.00.*

✗ **Jacob's on the Mall** 30A South Mall; ☎ 021 425 1530; e info@jacobsonthemall.com; www.jacobsonthemall.com [G3]. *Walk south down Marlboro St; when you reach South Mall, Jacob's will be just opposite.*

Located in the heart of Cork's financial district &, more decadently, in what used to be the Turkish Baths, this is where Cork's well-heeled set, & indeed everybody else, avail themselves of superb service, beautiful light-filled surrounds, diverse music (so diverse; truly a musical miscellany) & beautifully presented, scrumptious modern European food. My penne with parmesan cream sauce, bacon, broccoli, pine nuts & basil came adorned with great sheaves of pungent parmesan; I had to defend it physically from my dinner companion. Lunch starters include gem squash & thyme soup with smoked Gubbeen cheese as well as Ballycotton crab salad with ginger & lime mayonnaise, mango & basil dressing. Mains include a sirloin steak with garlic butter, caramelised onions, grilled flat mushrooms, chips & red wine jus. Dinner mains include teriyaki-marinated salmon with a crisp vegetable stir-fry & a divine basmati rice with lemon & raisins. (I have since implemented the lemon & raisin touch in my own cooking.) Desserts include baked peaches with vanilla ice cream & raspberry compôte & a pecan pie with caramel ice cream. The meals are made to order so if you are in a hurry or have any allergies, let them know. If you want to feel like royalty for an hour or two, look no further than Jacob's on the Mall. *Expensive; mains* **$$$$$**. *10% service charge on all bills in the evening. Open Mon–Sat, lunch 12.30–14.30, dinner 18.30–22.00. Closed Sun.*

✕ **Jacques Restaurant** 9 Phoenix St; ☎ 021 427 7387; e jacquesrestaurant@eircom.net; www.jacquesrestaurant.ie [G3]. *From the Grand Parade walk down Oliver Plunkett St, turn right at the GPO, take the next left; Jacques is on the left*
Run by Jacqueline & Eithne Barry, Jacques is one of Cork's longest-established restaurants, serving appetising food for over 25 years now. Tucked away on a little-known backstreet, it doesn't look like much on the outside, & to be honest the bare lightbulbs inside are not the most flattering or ambient either. The food, however, is a fabulous distraction. Kick off your meal with a half-bottle of sherry served with nuts & olives.

Starters include salads & seafood & soup but I think the colourful & well-presented antipasto will nicely whet your appetite for what is to come. As a main course try their stuffed breast of free-range chicken with warm gazpacho, basil, pine kernels & Italian-style potatoes. Their Early Bird menu comprises a starter & main course, the latter including fresh hake with caper & tomato salsa & summer vegetables; very very delicious. Desserts include a creamy lemon & mascarpone cheese tart. They also have a selection of reasonably priced meals for kids including chicken goujons with chips. The wine list is fab with a great selection of vintage wines & all the food is locally sourced. *Expensive; mains $$$$$. Open daily, dinner Mon–Sat 18.00–22.00 (last orders). Early Bird menu Mon–Sat 18.00–19.00.*

✗ **Les Gourmandises** 17 Cook St; ✆ 021 425 1959; e info@lesgourmandises.ie; www.lesgourmandises.ie [G3]

A discreet French bistro, Les Gourmandises should not be missed if an evening of subtle sophistication is what you require. Before you do anything at all, you can relax on their decadent red couches sipping an aperitif while you peruse their uncluttered à la carte menu which is pared down to choice dishes in each category. Starters range from Jerusalem artichoke soup with roasted chestnuts & thyme to marinated salmon with Brittany pancake, goat's cheese & organic rocket. If you are in any way unsure of what to go for, do not hesitate to ask the very obliging staff who are minor experts in every dish prepared on their premises as well as being extremely adept at sizing up what it is you are likely to enjoy. Main courses include roasted sea scallops with fennel puree, tapenade & lemon, or roasted fillet of beef with confit of red onions, wild mushrooms & thyme jus. Presentation is very artistic, you almost don't want to disturb the food. Meat-eaters are well-catered for, vegetarians not so well unfortunately. A vegetarian dish can be prepared upon request but there is no such option on the menu — kind of spoils the fun a little for the diner. The desserts are exquisite, for example vanilla crème brulée with poached pear & lemon financier (a sort of almond sponge cake). Their coffee crème brulée with Swiss meringue & chocolate madeleine is the best I have ever had. In a way it's sort of ruined me; I turn my nose up at all other crème brulées now. Their wine list is such that you want to photocopy it & send it off to every other restaurant in the city as an example of what a wine list should look like. So much about this restaurant is perfect. They also do a 3-course dinner menu (2 options in each category) from Tue–Thu which is quite good value & includes a glass of wine. *Expensive; mains* $$$$$. *Service charge of 10% for groups of 6 and over. Open Tue–Thu, set dinner & à la carte 18.00–22.00; Fri—Sat, set dinner 18.00–19.00, à la carte 19.00–22.00. Lunch on Fri only.*

✗ **The Liberty Grill** 32 Washington St; ☎ 021 427 1049; e dine@libertygrillcork.com; www.libertygrillcork.com [E3]
Burgers are the order of the day in this stylish little restaurant, although it's equally good if you've slept in late, missed the b/fast at your hotel & need something solid & breakfasty to sort out your hangover. B/fast menu includes muesli, yoghurt, fruit, scones, pastries, pancakes, eggs, 'posh toast' & all the makings of a good fry-up. Later on in the day you can choose from a range of salads or you can go for one of their burgers (bacon, haloumi, falafel, crab, lamb, chicken, tempeh, tuna, beef) all served with chips & with a range of side orders & extra toppings if you really want to go the whole hog. Desserts are good too; I recommend the maple yoghurt with crushed pecans & berry compote (heavy on the blackcurrants). Whitewashed stone walls & lots of greenery give this place a very fresh feel. The food is very good value & the staff are very friendly. *Mid-range; mains* $$$. *Breakfast 08.00–17.00, lunch 12.00–17.00, dinner – last orders 21.00.*

✗ **Luigi Malones** 1–2 Emmet Pl; ☎ 021 427 8877; e emmetplace@luigimalones.com; www.luigimalones.com [F2]

Ideal for coffee, lunch, dinner or cocktails, the Cork branch of Luigi's is art deco but unpretentious. You can sit outside, handy for the smokers, or you can opt for indoors where there are many comfortable seating arrangements, the best in my view being the few soft squishy leather seats just either side of the door as you come in. Luigi's is especially good value for lunch during the working week. They do a special menu which includes a glass of wine or a soft drink – a bargain for around a tenner. Service is friendly & efficient, the portions are generous & the house wines are particularly good. Being a chain, however, there's no sense of a chef's individuality or style. The chicken enchilada you have today will probably be identical in all respects to the chicken enchilada you have a year from now. As well as pastas & pizzas, there are sizzling fajitas (giant unfinishable portions), char-grilled hamburgers, steaks & a list of house specials including such varied dishes as aubergine & chicken tagine, seafood cataplana, lamb & chorizo espetadas, & firecracker prawns. The cocktail list is extensive, the margaritas are great when they get them right, & the dessert menu is pretty enticing too: the key lime & lemon cheesecake is very good. There are a couple of interesting artefacts worth noting in the Cork Luigi's. The first thing you see when you walk in the door is the large clock facing you. It is one of the original station clocks from King's Cross. One of the fans in the main dining area is a propeller from the first plane to cross the Atlantic. And just to prove that the name 'Luigi Malone' is not some hokey fusion construct, there is a photo of the man himself, on the 'family wall'. *Mid-range; mains* $$$. *Open daily 10.00–23.00.*

✗ **Proby's Bistro** Proby's Quay, Crosses Green; ☎ 021 431 6531; e info@probysbistro.com; www.probysbistro.com [E3]

Overlooked by St Finbarre's Cathedral, there is a warm summery feel to this small restaurant with its textured orange walls, shuttered windows & soft lighting. The food is diverse, encompassing Mediterranean & modern Irish cooking, & reasonably priced. You can avail yourself of their Early Bird menu which consists of two courses & a glass of wine for a very good price. I had their bruschetta with roasted Mediterranean vegetables & rocket pesto, all very satisfyingly smothered in melted mozzarella. My main course was a roast breast of chicken with red wine jus, scallion creamed potatoes & braised swede in which I think I detected a hint of mint. Not the most adventurous of meals, but certainly very filling. Also on offer are a spinach & ricotta tortellini tossed in basil & pine nut pesto with black olives & parmesan cheese, as well as baked fillet of cod, basil oil, sweet pepper mash & roast Mediterranean vegetables. Desserts include banoffi pie with raspberry coulis & chocolate & chestnut log with wild berry compote amongst others. Their à la carte has a far more extensive & interesting selection of dishes. A typical starter is the in-house smoked chicken & asparagus tartlet on a bed of braised leeks with a basil & white wine cream sauce. Mains include artichoke & pine nut risotto cooked with white wine & garlic & finished with smoked Gubbeen cheese. Desserts include such indulgences as Teacher's Scotch & black cherry cheesecake with winter berry coulis. Staff are friendly & the atmosphere is one of secluded comfort. The music is a little bland but at the very least it is kept in the background. *Above average; mains $$$$. Service charge of 10% for parties of 8 or more. Open for lunch Mon–Fri 12.00–17.00, open for dinner Mon–Sat 18.00–22.00. Early Bird menu Mon–Sat 18.00–19.30.*

✗ **Star Anise** 4 Bridge St; ✆ 021 455 1635; e staranise@eircom.net; staranise-cork.com [G2]
This is a warm stylish urbane little place that fills quickly. I recommend making a reservation if you have your heart set on eating there in the evening. Cruisey tunes carrying gently through the air, orange hues & amber candlelight softening the evening & the friendly professional staff make eating here a delight. A surprise taster of hot tomato & pesto in a shot glass kicked the evening off to a great start, as surprise tasters tend

to do. You can have a starter as a main course if such is your desire (you will be charged twice its starter price), & starters feature such filling dishes as grilled squid rings with chorizo & tomato salsa, & lamb, mint & cumin boreks (deep-fried spring rolls). Also on the menu was roasted pork belly with Chinese cabbage & spicy oriental sauce. The lunch menu varies from the familiar soup of the day to the sexier smoked venison with potato & chive salad & red pepper chutney. I like this place, maybe even more for the gorgeous interior & the sophisticated but friendly ambience than for the food, but the food is good too! *Expensive; mains* **$$$$$**. *Service charge of 10% for groups of 6 and over. Open Tues–Sat. Lunch Tue–Fri 12.00–15.00, dinner Tue–Sat 18.00–23.00. Early Bird menu Tue–Fri 18.00–19.00.*

✕ **Star Vast** 17 Princes St; ☎ 021 425 4969; f 021 425 4968 [G3]
Formerly known as Tao Tao & voted 'one of the one hundred best restaurants in Ireland 2003' by *The Times*, this Chinese restaurant & noodle bar is one of the most popular in Cork. I must confess to not liking Chinese food but I would eat here simply for the ambience & the décor. Modern, minimalist & subtly oriental with small bunches of carnations here & there, lots of rose & peach backlighting, cream & red walls — a few cherry blossoms floating through the air would not have been out of place. The menu is extensive, catering for meat-eaters, seafood-lovers & vegetarians alike. I recommend getting a starter as all the meals are freshly prepared so you may be waiting a while for your main course. Mains vary from shredded duck Cantonese (vermicelli rice noodle casserole) to an ambre fire fillet steak, a fiery dish consisting of beef fillet shreds marinated in a hot tomato chilli & stir-fried with julienne of peppers & fresh chillies. Several of the dishes are available as vegetarian options on request. The profiteroles for dessert are absolutely delicious as is the Tia Maria coffee. Star Vast also offer a take-away service. *Mid-range; mains* **$$$**. *Open Mon–Thu 12.00–22.00, Fri & Sat 12.00–23.00, Sun 16.00–22.00.*

✖ **Wagamama** 4–5 South Main St; ☎ 021 427 8874; www.wagamama.ie [E3]

Popular noodle bar chain with communal seating. Speedy service, tasty healthy Asian food. Lots of different kinds of noodles, varying degrees of spiciness, plenty of choice for both 'carnivores' & vegetarians. Take-away service available. *Mid-range; mains* **$$$**. *Open Mon–Sat 12.00–23.00, Sun 12.00–22.00.*

CAFÉS

✖ **Café Bar Deli** 18 Academy St; ☎ 021 485 1865; www.cafebardeli.ie [F2]

Irish chain serving Mediterranean food; quite a hip little place, always crowded. Typical dishes include penne amatriciana with pancetta, garlic & rosemary in a red wine, shallot & tomato sauce. The pizzas are also quite interesting; for example, harissa-spiced tomato sauce, mozzarella, paprika, tuna steak, green olives, red onion & scallions. There's a good selection of salads & the desserts aren't bad either. Always a buzzy atmosphere. There are entrances on both Academy St & French Church St. *Mid-range; mains* **$$$**. *Open Mon–Sat 12.00–23.00; Sun 12.30–22.00.*

✖ **The Crawford Café** The Crawford Art Gallery, Emmet Pl; ☎ 021 427 4415 [F2]

Centrally located, the Crawford Café is always packed at lunchtime. Quite an upmarket little place, the menu includes spinach & mushroom pancake with hollandaise sauce & salad as well as a pork, spinach & herb terrine with crusty white bread & salad. They also do a set lunch for around €25 consisting of soup, main course, dessert & tea/coffee. There's something nice about having lunch in an art gallery & the café lives up to its eminent surrounds. *Cheap & cheerful; mains* **$$**. *Open Mon–Sat 10.00–16.30.*

✕ The Farmgate Café Old English Market, Princes St Entrance; ☏ 021 427 8134 [F3]
Located on a balcony overlooking the market stalls & fountain, the Farmgate is a popular mid-shop stop & is ideal for people-watching. Here you'll find much of what is on offer downstairs cooked to perfection & ready to be devoured. One side is a self-service café with free coffee top-ups, the other a restaurant with table service (same food, same prices). There are plenty of traditional Irish dishes on offer, including the Cork specialities tripe & drisheen (see pages 98–9). They also have fabulous cakes, chief among them their banoffi pie. If it's cold outside, it'll be cold in the Farmgate too. Leave your coat on. *Cheap & cheerful; mains* $$. *Open Mon–Sat 09.00–17.30.*

✕ Gusto 3 Washington St; ☏ 021 425 4446; e info@cafegusto.com; www.cafegusto.com [F3]
One of the things I love about Gusto is that you can phone in your order & it will be ready for collection when you arrive. But even more than that I love their goat's cheese salad wraps. I've tried all their wraps (also available as rolls or salads), the Italian salad, the Thai chicken, the crispy Brie, & the chorizo Español amongst others but, in the firm opinion of myself & at least two other people, the goat's cheese salad wrap is the hands-down winner. Goat's cheese, roasted red peppers, a tangy red-onion marmalade, lettuce, hummus & tapenade, this is a succulent, tasty combination that I never ever tire of eating. For 50c extra you can have your wrap toasted – totally worth it. Gusto also have a decent range of coffees & teas available, some would say the best coffee in the city, & then there's the Indian chai in the winter, as well as a small selection of pastries & snacks. Decaf & low fat or soya milk are available on request. If you are going to be in Cork for an extended period of time it might be worth your while picking up one of their loyalty cards (free beverage after so many stamps). You can eat in or take away but really, I defy you to leave Cork without trying the goat's cheese salad wrap. They now have a second smaller branch on The Boardwalk on Lapp's Quay. *Cheap & cheerful; mains* $$. *Open Mon–Sat 07.45–18.00, food served until 17.00.*

💻 **Idaho** 19 Caroline St; ☎ 021 427 6376 [G2]

Another of Cork's cosy, tucked-away cafés, you almost wouldn't notice this peculiarly shaped, perched-on-a-corner gem as you stride down Maylor St past Caroline St. Small with dark wooden furniture, cream walls & red lampshades. I always feel I should be drinking mugs of mulled wine in there. A popular spot for b/fast, you can have, amongst others, hot Belgian waffles with organic maple syrup or piping-hot porridge with brown sugar & cream (delectable). Lunchtime is equally busy in there with several dishes to choose from including gratinated potato gnocchi with cream, smoky bacon & sage, or hashed potatoes with chorizo & smoked Irish brie. They also do soup as well as a selection of bapinis, each served with a side salad. It's the kind of place where you could linger all afternoon with a bottle of wine & indeed you are encouraged to do so. Sit yourself down under the mirror at the round table & survey the blackboard enumerating their range of wines. You won't want to leave, especially if it's raining & they're playing salsa music & you've spotted that for not very much money at all you can have a bowl of Cantuccini biscuits to dip in your coffee (free refills — added bonus). Recommended in both the Bridgestone & Jameson guides, Idaho is your man if you're looking for somewhere to while away a few hours. I just wish they opened on Sun too. *Cheap & cheerful; mains* $$. *Open Mon–Thu 08.30–17.00, Fri & Sat 08.30–18.00. B/fast 08.30–12.00, lunch 12.00–16.30.*

💻 **Insomnia** French Church St; ☎ 021 427 9701 [F2]

Part of a chain owned by Hughes & Hughes bookshop, this is an inviting café with comfortable arm-chairs, decent coffee & nice cakes. *Rock bottom; pastries* $. *Mon–Thu, Sat 08.00–18.00, Fri 08.00–20.00, Sun 12.00–18.00.*

💻 **Joup** Unit 4B, Old English Market; ☎ 086 877 6450 [F3]

Juice & soup — joup — brilliant! This is a very popular place & highly recommended. It's absolutely tiny & can seat about 10½ people but all their food is prepared for take-away, so don't worry if you can't get a seat. They also do a range of sandwiches & scones. The broccoli soup is very good. A simple concept — healthy, fresh, tasty food — but a winning one. Don't miss it. *Cheap & cheerful; mains* $$. *Open Mon–Sat, 09.00–17.30.*

💻 **Nosh + Coffee** Carey's La; ☎ 021 490 5877 [F2]
Dimly lit, friendly café in what you could call Cork's boho area. Divine chocolate muffins, Fairtrade coffee, wine by the glass, soups, ciabattas, bagels, baguettes, jacket potatoes; nice for food & nice for just sipping your latte & lounging about on their comfy couches. Good music. *Cheap & cheerful; mains* $$. *Open Mon–Thu, Sat 08.30–18.00, Fri 08.30–19.00, Sun 11.00–18.00.*

💻 **Puccinos** 9 Paul St, Rory Gallagher Pl; ☎ 021 427 1082; www.puccinos.com [F2]
Part of a chain, this bright & cheery café serves all manner of food & prides itself on the quality of its coffee. It's also a café with a sense of humour with pithy remarks coming at you from every angle — the walls, the menu, even the sachets. Baked potatoes, wraps, ciabattas, tapas, salads, pizzas, pastas (pizza for snobs apparently), it's a good place for mid-shop stop. Reasonably priced, friendly, ironic. *Cheap & cheerful; mains* $$. *Open Mon–Wed 09.30–18.30, Thu–Sat 09.30–21.00, Sun 10.00–18.00.*

💻 **The Quay Co-op** 24–5 Sullivan's Quay; ☎ 021 431 7026; e quaycoop@eircom.net; www.quaycoop.com [F3]
A popular vegetarian café spread over the two floors above their health shop (see page 148) & overlooking the Lee — the tables by the windows are invariably the first to go. Approaching the Quay Co-op in the evening from the Grand Parade, the turquoise walls of the first floor & the orange of the second shine out brightly & invitingly. They have a self-service system in operation & the walls behind the counter are covered

in blackboards, listing their innumerable dishes as well their codes indicating which of their dishes are wheat/dairy/sugar/nut/gluten-free etc. They have a large range of salads & hot dishes, eat-in or take-away, as well as an extensive selection of cakes & herbal teas. They are lovely surrounds in which to eat — bright walls on which paintings by local artists are often displayed, candles, plants & bunches of orchids, & of course the view from the windows. *Cheap & cheerful; mains* $$. *Open Mon–Sat 09.00–21.00. Closed Sun.*

💻 Sugar Café 25 Washington St West [E3]
Nice bright café, serving Fairtade coffee. Under the same ownership as Petits Fours, the patisserie a few doors up, & a lot of what you can buy in the patisserie is available in Sugar to consume on the spot with your hot beverage of choice. *Cheap & cheerful; mains* $$. *Open Mon–Fri 08.00–17.00.*

💻 Taste! The Rory Gallagher Café 4 Union Quay; ☏ 021 496 4900; e mail@taste.ie; www.taste.ie [H3]
Run by a Dutch couple who also run a Rory Gallagher concert in Leeuwarden in North Holland every year, Taste! is a treat for Rory fans & coffee-culture fans alike. Small & tastefully furnished, there are pictures & posters on the walls, many of which have been donated by Donal Gallagher, Rory's brother & manager, as well as a framed bandana that once belonged to Rory. On the food side of things, particularly popular are their Dutch pancakes, ideal for b/fast & very good value for money; try a seasons pancake — a large fruit-laden pancake featuring kiwis, oranges, peaches, cherries & cream. Very tasty & more filling than you'd think. Savoury pancakes are available also, as are full-Irish & full-Dutch breakfasts. Soup, sandwiches & toasties are also available, as are more substantial meals (named after Rory songs): for example, a Race the Breeze bap (salmon, capers, lemon & salad). You don't have to be a Rory fan to enjoy a coffee in Taste! Well worth checking out. *Cheap & cheerful; mains* $$. *Open Mon–Fri 08.00–16.00.*

Tribes 8 Tuckey St; ☎ 021 427 4446 [F3]

Popular with clubbers looking for that coffee hit before they blearily make their way home. Tribes serve a large range of coffees, teas & fruit infusions, wines & beers as well as various specials during the day, like lasagne & salad. Popular with school-goers during the day. *Rock bottom; mains* $. Open Mon–Wed 10.30–midnight, Thu–Sat 10.30–04.00, Sun 13.00–22.00.

Triskel Café 14a Tobin St; ☎ 021 427 4644 [F3]

Small, unpretentious (despite being part of an arts centre) café, that has the appearance of being full of natural light despite being situated on a very poky street. Very calm, with communal & individual tables as well as a couch; I think if I was the kind of writer who liked to do my writing on a laptop in a café (how do they concentrate?), this is where I would come. Serves the usual café fare, wraps, paninis, baked potatoes & the like. *Cheap & cheerful; mains* $$. Open Mon–Fri & Sun 09.30–17.00. Closed Sat.

Wild Ways 21 Princes St; ☎ 021 427 2199; e info @ wildways.net; www.wildways.net [G3]

A busy organic café situated right in the middle of town, it is a bright & cheery place for both b/fast & lunch. Eat-in or take-away, breakfasts include omelettes, scrambled eggs & porridge with berry compote – very reasonably priced considering they are all made from organic ingredients. Lunch includes a range of hot sandwiches, amongst them goat's cheese, tomato, red onion & sweetcorn on focaccia, or a marinated Mediterranean vegetable wrap with smoked Gubbeen cheese. All the sandwiches are served with a choice of either a baked potato or mixed-bean salad. See their board for their daily specials. *Cheap & cheerful; mains* $$. Open Mon–Fri 08.00–17.00, Sat 08.30–17.00. Breakfast 08.00–12.00, lunch 12.00–17.00.

BARS AND PUBS SERVING FOOD

Lots of pubs serve food at lunchtime but the following are either on that hazy bar/café divide or are worth mentioning for not confining their menu to traditional pub grub.

♀ **The Long Island** 11–12 Washington St; ☎ 021 427 3252 [F3]
I'm more inclined to recommend this place for its cocktails (see page 129) but I think their lunch menu is also worth a mention. With a range of soups & toasted sandwiches, large portions ensure that you will not leave the bar with any space for dessert. There are a few comfy couches dotted around the place & large, tall tables. *Cheap & cheerful; mains $$. Open pub hours, food available Mon–Fri 12.00–15.00.*

♀ **The Long Valley** Winthrop St; ☎ 021 427 2144 [G3]
I think the Long Valley has a special place in many people's hearts. It has something of a literary reputation, the kind of place where you supposedly see scruffy types sitting in corners scribbling furiously (although I never have) but really I think it's their Toasted Special that keeps the lunchtime punters coming back. Nothing more fussy than a toasted sandwich with ham, cheese, tomato & onion (sachets of mustard etc available on the tables), they are yum & deserve their long-standing reputation. Served to you by busy ladies in white coats, it all smacks of simpler, less-pretentious times & the tea comes in large pots which always gets a thumbs-up from me. *Rock bottom; mains $. Open pub hours, food available till 15.00.*

♀ **Meade's Wine Bar** 126 Oliver Plunkett St; ☎ 021 427 1530 [G3]
It's very easy to walk right past this comfortably dark wine/tapas bar without ever noticing it, but once you

do find it, you know you've really discovered something. Very nice wines, very nice food, tapas, cheeses, sushi, desserts. Lots for the discerning taste bud. *Mid-range; mains* $$$. *Open from 18.00 Tue–Sun.*

♀ **Soho** 77 Grand Parade; ☎ 021 422 4040; e info@soho.ie; www.soho.ie [F3]
Prime location on Grand Parade, this bar/restaurant looks like it's been airlifted out of the South Mall, replete with men in suits, although the graffiti on the walls inside suggests that they're aiming for a broader clientele. Nevertheless, it has a slightly more upmarket feel, even though its lunches (Creole chicken salad, seafood chowder, to name but a couple) are competitively priced. Lunch is served in the bar on the ground floor, while dinner is served in the restaurant upstairs. *Lunch cheap & cheerful; mains* $$; *dinner mid-range; mains* $$$.

♀ **The Woodford Bourne** 19–20 Paul St; ☎ 021 425 3932; e info@thewoodford.ie; www.thewoodford.ie [F2]
Come lunchtime this is a popular spot; sometimes you may have to wait for a table, but it is quite a large place & they can usually fit you in. This is another eaterie that's all armchairs & couches so you'll find yourself settling in very quickly. They have an à la carte menu as well as a soup & sandwich bar where you can get a substantial Cajun chicken ciabatta served with a side salad for a reasonable sum. It's good value, the food is tasty, & the surroundings are comfortable. My only quibble with the place is that the pots of tea are minuscule. *Mid-range; mains* $$$. *Open for coffee from 10.00, food served 12.00–19.00.*

TAKE-AWAYS

🍽 **The Berries** 42 MacCurtain St; ☎ 021 450 9270; e info@theberries.ie; www.theberries.ie [G2]
Very friendly juice & coffee bar with an extensive range of juices (juicy lucy), smoothies (go smooth), frappes,

coffees, teas (hotties) & organic & gluten-free snacks. For b/fast try a strekkie: muesli, strawberries, honey, yoghurt & milk. Wash it down with a juicy lucy, for example, a blapple (apple & blueberry) to which you can add echinacea, spirulina, rhodiola or linseed if you want it to be extra healthy. *Rock bottom; drinks* $. *Open Mon–Fri 08.00–19.00, Sat 10.00–18.00, Sun 12.00–18.00.*

✗ Fast Al's Pizza Slice Café Corner of Castle St & South Main St [E3]

Open at unpredictable hours & largely catering for the drinking masses in the middle of the night, Fast Al's serves up a decent slice of pizza for roughly the price of a pint. Garlic bread is also available as is a small selection of gourmet rolls & wraps. Falaf Al's is next door if you fancy a change from pizza.

⌨ L.A. Bagels Oliver Plunkett St; ☎ 021 427 2796 [G3]

Serving bagels (surprise, surprise), wraps, salad bowls & soups. B/fast bagels include Nutella & banana, more savoury bagels include 'the classic' – Irish smoked salmon & cream cheese seasoned with fresh lemon juice & ground pepper, with or without capers (with, surely!). All the bagels are also available as wraps & there are lots of bagel flavours, everything from sun-dried tomato to cinnamon & raisin. All freshly baked on the day. *Rock bottom; mains* $.

✗ Lennox's Bandon Rd; ☎ 021 431 6118 [D4]

So famous are Jackie Lennox's fish 'n' chips in Cork, that a rival chipper opened up a very similar take-away in the city centre & named itself Lennox's too, hoping, I assume, to cash in on the name & reputation. But the truth soon got out. I'm sure they do a fine chip, but the Lennox's I'm choosing to champion today is the one on Bandon Road. In operation for over 50 years now, Ireland's first purpose-built chipper has been dishing out all manner of potato products to long but fast-moving queues of hungry Corkonians with roaring success.

No anaemic little French fries here, but solid 3-D 100% Irish potato chips. *Rock bottom; mains $. Open noon–01.00.*

✖ **The Spice Route** 35 MacCurtain St; ☎ 021 450 8382 [G2]
You can eat-in here but the lighting is neon & everything is plastic. It detracts from the food a little, which is very tasty indeed as well as being reasonably priced. They have several menus — appetisers, side dishes, tandoori, balti, biryani, vegetarian, beef, chicken, lamb & prawn — each with several dishes on offer. They also do snack boxes, burgers, chips & kebabs. I recommend the Chicken Bhuna Masala. *Cheap & cheerful; mains $$. Open Mon–Wed 17.00–01.00, Thu–Sun 17.00–03.00.*

RESTAURANTS WITH A TAKE-AWAY SERVICE

✖ **Banna Thai** (see page 89)
✖ **Bombay Palace** (see page 90)
✖ **Indian Palace** (see pages 97–8)
✖ **Quay Co-op** (see pages 111–12)
✖ **Star Vast** (see page 107)
✖ **Wagamama** (see page 108)

FURTHER AFIELD

✖ **Ballymaloe House** Shanagarry, East Cork; ☎ 021 465 2531; e res@ballymaloe.ie; www.ballymaloe.com
By car, about 30km (40 mins) east of Cork city. Take the N25 following signs for Whitegate & Cloyne. The restaurant is 9km south of the N25, 3km beyond Cloyne (signposted)

Old-world country-house charm is epitomised by the world-renowned Ballymaloe House. Founded by Myrtle Allen roughly 40 years ago, Ballymaloe has long been a pioneer of locally sourced ingredients. They grow most of their own herbs & vegetables out of which the most sumptuous meals are created, where the emphasis is on bringing out the best in each disparate element of the dish. Rich & creamy, this is not diet fodder by any means. Sunday lunch is a buffet & is a great way to spend an afternoon. The dinner menu depends on the day you go. During the week the menu consists of several courses, after which I recommend you not move for a few hours. On Friday nights dinner starts with an hors d'oeuvre buffet including freshly caught shellfish & on Sunday nights the entire meal is served as a buffet. Set in beautiful surroundings with gardens & orchards & croquet, Ballymaloe — championing quality Irish produce & modern Irish cooking — is well worth a visit. They also run a guesthouse (see pages 78–9) as well as a cookery school (*www.cookingisfun.ie*) where you can do a 12-week certificate course. If you don't have time for this you can always attend one of their demonstrations which take place most weekdays 14.00–16.30. *Expensive; mains* $$$$$. *Open Tue–Sun 19.00–21.00 & Sun 12.30–14.00.*

�֬ Bunnyconnellan Myrtleville; ☎ 021 483 1213

Buses from Cork city to either Myrtleville or Fountainstown. If you get off in Fountainstown you can walk along the coast to Bunny's, enjoying the views & whetting your appetite. By car, head for Carrigaline; signposted from there
Location, location, location is what makes Bunnyconnellan (or Bunny's, as it's known locally) worth enduring a 12-mile bumpy bus ride or maybe even getting lost if you're driving (all part of the adventure?). A bar, restaurant & beer garden situated on a cliff overlooking the sea; they also have barbecues during the summer. The cosy pub has a nautical feel with its barometers & large hand-held lanterns, while dining in the restaurant conjures up dining on the *Titanic* — waves crashing outside, flowery wallpaper, gilt-edged oval mirrors, black-&-white framed photos, along with traditional Irish music. The food would also make a worthy last supper. Starters

include a selection of fresh, fully garnished seafood. The vegetarian mains include an asparagus, leek & carrot crumble, or vegetable crêpes glazed with a cheese sauce. Seafood dishes range from poached salmon to deepfried scampi in a tartare sauce. If you fancy something meatier, you could try duckling in orange & ginger sauce. Delicious desserts include a mouth-watering lemon & lime cheesecake with raspberry coulis & fresh strawberries & cream when they are available. All in all, a rewarding meal for having made the journey, especially if you walked any of it. Fabulous, if a bit chaotic, in summer & wonderfully melodramatic in winter. *Above average; mains* $$$$. *Restaurant open every evening from 19.00. Also open for Sun lunch.*

If you're venturing further afield in the west Cork direction, keep an eagle-eye out for **Ozhaven** (restaurant; *www.ozhaven.com*) in Oysterhaven and **Otto's Creative Catering** (restaurant and accommodation; *www.ottoscreativecatering.com*) on the coast outside Bandon.

DRINKING

Everyone knows the importance of the pub to Irish culture, and it may come as a surprise to some to discover that they are generally nothing like the often awful Irish Pubs abroad. A mangled 'Fields of Athenry' is often to be heard in the small hours of the morning as tone-deaf carousers make their way home, but it's seldom enough that you'll hear the song actually being played in a pub. Nor do we have pub chains with dodgy 'Oirish' names like Kitty O'Shea's and Bridie O'Reilly's. Staff aren't generally required to wear loud tartan outfits, whether or not Guinness travels well is not an issue and punters don't complain about the two-part pour 'taking too long'. And of course in Cork, Murphy's, not Guinness, is the stout of choice. If stout isn't your thing, there are lots of foreign beers available as well as some English ales.

DRINKING HOURS Pubs are open Monday to Thursday 10.30–23.30 plus 30 minutes drinking-up time, Friday and Saturday 10.30–00.30 plus 30 minutes, and Sunday noon–23.00 plus 30 minutes. Pubs with bar extensions open till 01.30 plus 30 minutes. All pubs are closed Christmas Day and Good Friday. Christmas Eve and Holy Thursday have midweek opening hours. If a Sunday is followed by a bank holiday it will have Saturday opening hours. Remember that it is against the law to smoke in pubs (see page 51).

PUBS Many people let their music taste determine their choice of pub, be it traditional Irish music, indie, salsa, dance, drum 'n' bass, whatever, and many more look for live music as an accompaniment to their 'pint of plain'. Some prioritise the size of the television screen showing the latest football matches, others are thinking of the salsa and tango classes going on upstairs. Some want to go somewhere glamorous where they can drink cocktails and pose, others don't care where they go so long as alcohol is served. Some just want a quiet pint, and maybe a few comedy sketches, others just want a shave. There are *loads* of pubs in Cork – I've listed just a fraction of them here. There is little point in categorising pubs according to budget as by and large prices are fairly uniform – nowhere is especially cheap. Instead I've grouped them according to area to facilitate those embarking on pub crawls, although considering how compact the city is, this is almost redundant, and I've tried to include at least one of every type of pub – the trad pub, the sports pub and so on – to assist those with particular pub needs!

MacCurtain – Coburg – Devonshire streets

Dan Lowrey's Tavern 13 MacCurtain St; ☎ 021 450 5071 [G2]
There's something typically Irish about this place. You walk in the door, all heads turn to see who's coming in, the eye-catching upholstery catches your eye. It's almost rural. Stained-glass windows, antique mirrors, fake open fire at the back with a few books on Ireland stacked nearby, lots of locals; drinking here is all about the pint & the conversation. They also serve lunch during the day 12.00–15.00.

The Corner House 7 Coburg St; ☎ 021 450 0655 [G2]
A popular lively pub, with a traditional element to it. Live music – bluegrass every Mon & Tue, trad on Wed.

Sin É 8 Coburg St; ☎ 021 450 2266 [G2]
This is one of the most individual pubs in Cork in that once upon a time it was also, in its spare time, a barber's. Every so often you could have a pint & a haircut for a special price. At the time of writing they had actually stopped the salon side of things, but you never know, they might resume it some day. One of

the things I liked about the Sin É was that it was a novelty pub without actually trying to be. You could very easily rock in & out of the place without ever knowing anything about its hirsutical sideline. Nevertheless it is quite a cool pub. Bright red walls, candlelit tables, fairylit bar, & barber chairs (& you thought they were just for lounging around in) upstairs. It's the kind of pub that has a very devout following; sometimes I get the impression that many of the clientele actually live there. The Sin É (translates as 'that's it', in Irish, pronounced 'shin ay') is also a great place to check out live music with trad sessions most evenings.

🍺 **The Abbot's Ale House** 17 Devonshire St; ☎ 021 450 7116 [G2]
A small brightly lit pub with a cosy fireplace, the foreign beers & unusual glasses are what set this pub apart. Large blackboards list the European (predominantly Belgian) beers, their alcohol content & price. Delirium Tremens, Floris Chocolate, Leffe — they're all here, they're all tasty, they all get you drunk very quickly & give murderous hangovers, so be careful!

Patrick – Winthrop – Phoenix – Oliver Plunkett streets
🍺 **Mutton Lane Inn** 3 Mutton La, Patrick St; ☎ 021 427 3471 [F3]
Tucked away on the rather dodgy-looking Mutton Lane (running off Patrick St, next to Oasis), the Mutton Lane Inn is like a murky but funky Long Valley (see next entry). A former old man's pub with its snugs & gloom & candles, it is owned by the same people who own the unconventional Sin É & the re-upholstered Oval & so also attracts a more offbeat younger drinker. It's perfect for dashing in out of the rain for an afternoon pint. An atmospheric pub in the heart of the city with a music collection ranging from Kate Bush to Bob Marley.

🍺 **The Long Valley** Winthrop St; ☎ 021 427 2144 [G3]
As well as being popular for its toasted sandwiches (see page 114), the Long Valley is a great pub for the

sinking of pints. A long, narrow pub with a black-&-white tiled floor, there are always plenty of people in there but it never feels too claustrophobic. Popular with young & old alike, it's a more traditional sort of pub but very much retains its own character.

🍺 Crane Lane Theatre Phoenix St; ☎ 021 427 8487 [G3]

One of the more recent & amibitious additions to the ever-changing Cork pub scene, the spacious Crane Lane Theatre aims to be a pub, a live music venue (see page 138) & even a nightclub (see page 131) on occasion. The décor is impressive, with good attention to detail — red curtains, stage door signs — a lot of thought has been put into the look of the place, not unusual considering it is under the same ownership as the Mutton Lane Inn, the Sin É & the Oval, some of the most popular pubs in Cork city. Smokers will be delighted with the heatred outdoor terrace & its retractable roof. There is a good range of drinks on offer: Belgian, German & Czech beers, English & Australian ales, organic cider, & Swedish pear cider to name but a few. Mid-week entertainment can include anything from jazz to trad to cabaret. At the time of writing they were about to launch a Myspace webpage.

🍺 The Old Oak 113 Oliver Plunkett St; ☎ 021 427 6165 [G3]

Fairly spacious pub; live music, lively, slightly older crowd. Gigs upstairs in Cyprus Avenue.

🍺 The HiB 108 Oliver Plunkett St (opposite the GPO); ☎ 021 427 2758 [G3]

This is a great pub, & completely unlike any other I've ever been in. It's very easy to miss the HiB (short for Hibernian) as it is on the second floor between Hogan's newsagents & Minihan's pharmacy. The entrance isn't very promising with its glaring light bulb, old staircase & torn fleur-de-lys wallpaper, but the tiny pub itself is the closest you'll get to drinking in a sitting-room without actually being invited into someone's home. Bob Dylan on the stereo, a mobile phone ban, couches, homely curtains, & framed pencil-portraits of famous people, signed & often accompanied by letters to the artist & proprietor Brian O'Donnell; this is a quirky pub with a reputation for tossing out those it takes a dislike to.

Ɛ **An Bróg** 74 Oliver Plunkett St; ☎ 021 427 1392 [F3]
Formerly a small grungy pub popular with students, An Bróg is now a large grungy pub popular with students — & those who want to continue their drinking into the small hours without going to a club. An Bróg (pronounced 'on brogue', meaning 'The Shoe') is open until 02.00 & consequently is always jammed. The later you are, the more likely it is that you will have to queue to get in. A loud & lively spot with a deliberately downbeat décor, the pub specialises in alternative & indie music, but they also have traditional Irish music sessions on Sun & Mon.

Paul – Castle – Cornmarket streets

♀ **The Woodford Bourne** 19–20 Paul St; ☎ 021 425 3932 [F2]
As well as catering for one's ciabatta needs (see page 115), the Woodford is also a busy bar in its own right. More selective about its clientele in the evenings (simply wearing sandals can be enough to be refused entry), it attracts an after-work business crowd, & with its soft lighting & comfortable chairs, it expects its target punter to behave in a dignified manner.

Ɛ **The Roundy** 1 Castle St; ☎ 021 427 7682 [F2]
Funky & urban, the Roundy went through a phase of being known as the Rhino Rooms, but it has finally acknowledged that it is round but proud (it's located on a corner) & has gone back to being called the

Roundy. They've also got round tables, while we're on the subject. It looks like it is the preserve of the glam & sophisticated, but like much else in Cork, it is far more down to earth than that. Another ex-old man's pub, it used to have curved whitewashed walls, which I liked, but for some reason the outside walls have now been painted cream. Never mind. The Roundy's eclectic music sounds, low couches & illuminated pink wall-panels give the place a very relaxed vibe. Upstairs they have a DJ churning out the tunes.

🍺 **Dennehy's** 11 Cornmarket St; ☎ 021 427 2343 [F2]
Another old man's pub with zero pretensions, Dennehy's is small, cosy & local. Full of regulars, there's always a friendly atmosphere in there.

North Mall
🍺 **The Franciscan Well Brewery** 14 North Mall; ☎ 021 439 3434; e info@franciscanwellbrewery.com; www.franciscanwellbrewery.com [D2]
Tired of drinking the same old beers the world over? Then this brew pub is for you. The Franciscan Well in the heart of the city brew their own lagers, stouts, wheat beers & ales & also have numerous foreign beers for sale as well as all the usual suspects. Try their Rebel Red (an ale) or Blarney Blonde (a lager), their Shandon Stout or their Friar Weisse wheat beer & what's more, drink it outside in their beer garden. If it's a sunny day this place will be mobbed, but if you don't mind sitting on the ground then there shouldn't be a problem. With barbecues every Thu during the summer, there's no excuse for not lining your stomach when trying out these slightly stronger-than-average bevvies. Built on the site of an old Franciscan monastery & well dating back to 1219, the water from the well supposedly had curative properties & people travelled from all over to drink from it. Not sure if there's much in the way of healing going on there any more but

the drinking is certainly still popular. Following the Bavarian Law of Brewing which states that only four ingredients may be used (water, hops, yeast & malt) in the brewing of beer, the Franciscan Well is possibly the only pub in Cork where you'll get a vegetarian pint, as most stouts contain a fish gelatin rendering them not purely vegetarian. With live music on Mon evenings, the Well is always worth checking out, especially in Oct when it hosts its annual October Beer Fest (see page 36–7) & around Apr when they have an Easter Beer Fest (see page 30). From Fri to Sun, in both cases, you can pack yourself into their thronged heated outdoor tent & choose from over 15 beers on tap as well as many more bottled beers, using their barbecued fare for soakage.

Liberty – South Main – Tuckey streets

🍺 **Cleavers** 7 Liberty St; ↘ 021 490 5990 [E3]
A tiny little pub on the site of a former butcher's, it is relatively new but no less popular than its more established counterparts. Small & intimate with a very hip vibe, a good spot to spend an evening if you manage to get seats.

🍺 **The Castle Inn** South Main St [E3]
Next door to The Raven, this is the last real country pub in the city. No kowtowing attempt has been made at modernisation: there's a counter, a few stools, normal 100 watt bulbs (none of your mood lighting), straightforward drinks (nothing blue or modish), & plenty of thirsty punters.

🍺 **The Raven** Paradise Pl, 100 South Main St; ↘ 021 427 7307 [E3]
Another dingy old man's pub revamped as a funky night spot, trendy without being too pretentious. It's small, blue & U-shaped with unobtrusive hanging baskets, copper lampshades, large windows & an enormous pre-

Raphaelite painting of *Hylas and the Nymphs* on its back wall. A good range of beers on tap, good tunes (lounge by day, beats by night), & always a good crowd.

♀ **Suas** 4–5 South Main St; e info@suasbar.com; www.suasbar.com [E3]
Rooftop bar (suas is Irish for 'up') located above Captain America's. Specialises in cocktails. I think the main draw with this place is the outdoor decking overlooking South Main St. Popular with smokers for obvious reasons.

🍺 **The Oval** Corner of South Main St & Tuckey St [E3]
The Roundy has returned & The Oval (so-named because of the shape of the ceiling, as far as I know) has had a slight makeover (it's now owned by the same person who owns the Sin É & the Mutton Lane Inn). This is a small but popular student pub. It was always a cool, fairly grungey place but now it's bordering on downright lovely. Smart upholstering has perked it up & made it more comfortable than ever. Loud alternative music draws in a large crowd of regulars & in the winter months the fireplace at the back keeps them there.

🍺 **An Spailpín Fánach** 27–9 South Main St; ✆ 021 427 7949 [E3]
Formerly a small pub, now quite large, it still retains its small-pub feel with all its nooks & crannies. There's something typically Irish about the Spailpín (translates as 'the wandering wayfarer', pronounced 'on spolpeen fawnock') with its worn wooden décor, its snugs & its traditional live music (every night except Sat). It's the kind of pub that puts you in the mood either for a pint or a hot port.

♀ **The Quad** 18 Tuckey St; ✆ 021 425 1456 [F3]
Another alternative music bar popular with students, they also have a large screen for live Premiership matches. *Open late Mon–Sun, closes at 02.00.*

Sullivan's Quay – Barrack – Tower – Douglas streets

Sober Lane Sullivan's Quay; ☎ 021 467 7217 [F3]
Named after a nearby laneway, Sober Lane is a popular addition to the Cork pub scene, with a friendly atmosphere & a young crowd. Pizza served till 23.00, regular live music, table quizzes on Tue, & a smoking room.

The Gateway 125 Barrack St; ☎ 021 431 5378 [E4]
The oldest pub in Cork, & possibly the oldest in Ireland (see page 162), the Gateway is still getting it on with the best of them. Old pub, young crowd – a busy place.

Tom Barry's 113 Barrack St [E4]
A small pub with a loyal local following, they also have a lovely beer garden out the back which is prettily lit with fairylights & colourful flowers during the summer.

Loafers 26 Douglas St; ☎ 021 431 1612 [G4]
Gay bar with a beer garden. Since the government smoking ban, the importance of beer gardens cannot be emphasised enough! See page 133.

An Crúiscín Lán 18–20 Douglas St; ☎ 021 431 6428 [H4]
Student pub, alternative music. The name translates as 'the full jug' & is pronounced 'on crooshkeen lawn'. Lots of gigs (lots of tribute bands) & singer-songwriter nights. If you want to catch some live music, it's worth keeping an eye on this place.

Union Quay

⌂ **Beale Street Blues Bar** 3 Union Quay; ☎ 021 496 4900; e annetspijker@eircom.net; www.bealestreetcork.com [H3]

Named after Beale Street in Memphis which is host to numerous blues bars & cafés, the Beale Street Blues Bar is an homage to blues & rock. The owners, Klaas & Annet Spijker, moved to Cork from Holland a few years ago & opened up Taste! The Rory Gallagher Café (see page 112) which is next door to Beale Street. The blues bar is their latest enterprise & is located in what used to be The Phoenix. Regular gigs feature a range of international blues musicians & there are even afternoon sessions to accommodate the younger fans.

⌂ **Charlie's** 2 Union Quay; ☎ 021 496 5272 [H3]

Another one of those dingy but cool pubs, good for live trad sessions, especially Sun afternoons. An early house, Charlie's is open from 07.00.

Washington Street – Lancaster Quay

♉ **The Long Island** 11–12 Washington St; ☎ 021 427 3252 [F3]

Not a bad place for lunch (see page 114), the cocktails are the Long Island's real reason for being. Try my favourite, the Caipirinha – fresh crushed limes & raw cane sugar buried in crushed ice & soaked in Cachaça, the Brazilian cane spirit. It will keep you on your toes.

⌂ **Preachers** Washington St; ☎ 085 742 9702 [E3]

Tiny pub selling pitchers of beer. Always packed; get here early if you want a seat. Indie tunes, studenty clientele.

🍺 **The Washington Inn** 30–31 Washington St; ☎ 021 427 3666 [E3]
A student pub known more commonly as The Wash, it's always loud & crowded & you may have to queue to get in. Chart music is the order of the day.

🍺 **Reardens** 26 Washington St; ☎ 021 427 1969; www.reardens.com [E3]
Hugely popular, loud & lively. You may have to queue to get in here. Live music every Wed, Fri & Sun from 22.30. Tues are retro with '70s & '80s music from 22.00 till late. Scruffy attire will see you turned away by their no-nonsense bouncers, as will baggy trousers & trainers.

🍺 **Costigan's** 11 Washington St West; ☎ 021 427 3350 [E3]
Another busy pub along this strip. Similar ambience, similar clientele. Chart music, students, young professionals.

🍷 **Reidy's Wine Vault** Opposite Jury's Hotel, Western Rd; ☎ 021 427 5751 [D3]
A popular student/thespian hangout, Reidy's is the closest & most capacious watering hole for the cast & audience of whatever's just been on in the nearby Granary Theatre (see pages 135–6).

POOL/BOWLING
🍺 **Mardyke** Sheares St; ☎ 021 427 3000; www.mardyke.com [D3]
If you're not in the mood for traipsing from bar to bar & are looking for a slightly more active night out, the Mardyke isn't the prettiest or most atmospheric of bars, but it does have a bowling alley, 17 pool tables, the beer is as good as anywhere else & they serve food.

7 Entertainment and Nightlife

NIGHTCLUBS

As a student city, there are nightclubs catering for pretty much every taste in music and ambience. Monday and Tuesday nights are the only real quiet nights. Wednesday to Sunday there's lots going on.

☆ **Crane Lane Theatre** Phoenix St; ☎ 021 427 8487 [G3]
At the time of writing Crane Lane Theatre (see pages 123 & 138) was not yet operating as a nightclub, but there were plans to hold alternative/indie club nights in the live music room.

☆ **Freakscene at Qube and The Works** Oliver Plunkett St; www.freakscene.com [F3]
Freakscene is a Cork institution. Just over 12 years old it is Ireland's longest-running club night & is now in its fifth home, The Qube/Works. It started off in the infamous Sir Henry's, once voted one of the best clubs in Europe in an MTV poll & to my mind Freakscene's best venue ever & indeed Cork's best club. Unfortunately Henry's has closed down & no club since has managed to pull off that dingy underground feel that Henry's bandied about with such reckless abandon. And so Freakscene has become something of a nomad. An alternative club, it takes place every Wed night & always has a second room, Danascene, where DJs Jenny Glitt & Velma Velour delight their cult following with Kate Bush & Abba & sundry other offbeat tunes. Both the Scenes are

great & The Qube is an adequate venue for the time being. Entry is only €5 & the lollipops are free! Check out their lively website for all the up-to-the-minute info & reviews on alternative music & clubbing in Cork.

☆ **Kickback** Everyman Palace Theatre, 15 MacCurtain St; ✆ 021 450 1673 [H2]
Hailed by many as the best nightclub in Cork at the moment. It's not really a nightclub, it's a theatre, but there's music (funk, soul, salsa, whatever takes the DJ's fancy) & late-night dancing & cocktail-drinking every Fri night from 23.30 (the first hour is Happy Hour) in the Everyman bar & foyer. It's Fri night; what else are you going to do apart from kick back? Great fun, go there.

☆ **The Savoy** Patrick St; ✆ 021 425 1419; www.savoycork.com [G2]
Formerly a cinema (like so many buildings in Cork), this capacious nightclub very much has its finger on the musical pulse. Tue & Thu: Bang — ance, funk, soul, r&b, indie, quite a studenty night out. Fri: Twist — disco, soul, r&b, hip hop. Sat: Rapture — very popular, DJs playing r&b, soul, house, hiphop & live bands playing all sorts of everything. A good night out. One Wed a month: Knock Knock Club — live music in the Savoy mezzanine, an intimate atmospheric venue. The Savoy is, generally speaking, one of the key live music venues for international acts; there's always something going on there.

GAY/LESBIAN

Cork's gay scene has improved slightly over the last few years. There are still not that many gay pubs and clubs but there are at least a few to choose from. Many other bars and clubs consider themselves gay-friendly. The website www.gaycork.com is useful for finding out about forthcoming events. The following are all in the city centre

☆ **Climax at The Liquid Lounge** Marlborough St (above Clancy's bar) [G3]
Fashionable gay club night in The Liquid Lounge one Sat a month.

☆ **Instinct** Sullivan's Quay; ☎ 021 496 6726; www.instinctbarcork.com [F3]
Instinct used to be located just off Patrick St, & the new venue has gone down well with some while others miss the original. By & large it's a popular bar, draws quite a young crowd; there's a small cover charge at the weekends. Tue night is comedy night.

☆ **Loafers Bar** 26 Douglas St; ☎ 021 431 1612; www.loafersbar.com [G4]
A popular laid-back bar with a nice beer garden, it is actually Ireland's oldest gay bar. Generally more popular with women than men. Draws a slightly older crowd. The UCC Gay & Lesbian Society often meet here.

☆ **The Other Place** 8 South Main St; ☎ 021 427 8470; e info@theotherplaceclub.com; www.gayprojectcork.com [E3]
A resource centre & a nightclub, The Other Place is Cork's most well-established gay club. The nightclub is no longer open every weekend; instead it is now open on the first Sat of every month & for special events. Entry is from St Augustine's St just off South Main St. There is, however, a late bar & DJ every Sat night. The resource centre is home to the Southern Gay Health Project, a small bookshop & a drop-in centre where you can make tea/coffee. The Other Place Café is now open for b/fast & also has an Early Bird menu available.

Wed night is Movie Night, with a different film shown every week at 19.30. They also provide free wireless broadband access. You can either bring your own laptop or use one provided by the café. *Open Mon–Fri 10.00–22.00, Sat (non-club nights) 10.00–01.00 (late bar), Sun 12.00–18.00.*

THEATRE AND OPERA

☙ Corcadorca Theatre Company www.corcadorca.com

This is a listing of theatres but I am including this particular theatre company here because they often don't perform in theatres at all, but in public spaces, thus creating their very own 'venue' as it were. They regularly commission new writing & look to engage their public by producing work specific to sites of cultural significance within the city centre, which they then perform on-site. This kind of innovation leaves no room for a complacent audience. If you have any interest in theatre, you should definitely try & catch one of their performances.

☙ Cork Opera House Emmet Pl; ☎ 021 427 4308; bookings: 021 427 0022; ℮ info@corkoperahouse.ie; www.corkoperahouse.ie [F2]

The only purpose-built opera house in the country today (see pages 179–80), opera forms only one part of its programme of entertainments. Concerts, pantomimes, dance, comedy, film, cabaret, drama, gigs, musicals & festivals all find an outlet in the Opera House. Conventional perhaps, but the productions are usually of a high quality. There is a café on the ground floor as well as 2 very modern & comfortable bars on the second & third floors respectively, both of which have glass walls affording magnificent views of the city & the River Lee. See & be seen. Phone lines open Mon–Sat 09.00–19.00, counter open Mon–Sat 09.00–17.30 (9.00–19.00 on performance nights). Discounts for groups over 20. Concessions available to unwaged, full-time third-level students & OAPs. Discounts are not available for concerts. Wheelchair accessible. Induction loop in operation on ground floor for patrons with hearing difficulties.

🎭 **Everyman Palace Theatre** 15 MacCurtain St; ☏ 021 450 1673; e info@everymanpalace.com; www.everymanpalace.com [H2]

A 630-seat Victorian theatre, it is housed in a listed building steeped in character. Their programme is the usual mix of plays, operas, musicals & concerts with a particular emphasis on Irish drama. They usually stage three in-house productions a year under the direction of the theatre's artistic director. Every Christmas they have an immensely popular five-week pantomime & during the summer they specialise in Irish productions. They have 2 bars & it is worth bearing in mind that you can pre-order your drinks so you don't have to spend any intervals queuing & jostling for the barman's attention. Box office open Mon–Sat 10.00–19.30 (10.00–18.00 on non-performance days), Sun 14.00–19.30 (performance days only).

🎭 **Granary** Dyke Parade; ☏ 021 490 4275; e info@granary.ie; www.granary.ie [C3]

Providing teaching, rehearsal & performance space, Granary (funded by UCC) is a hive of both student & professional activity. Drama, dance, music, art, installations, workshops, talks, presentations – there are experimental, inter-disciplinary & contemporary performances year-round in this modern theatre.

CINEMA

City centre cinema would appear to be on the decline with many people now flocking to various suburban muliplexes for their helping of Hollywood. This, despite a thriving annual film festival.

The Gate Multiplex North Main St; ☎ 021 427 9595; www.corkcinemas.com or www.entertainmentireland.ie [E2]
Mainstream cinema, programmes run from Fri–Thu. Their flyers & ticket stubs are often worth hanging onto as they regularly entitle you to a certain percentage off a meal in a particular restaurant or a free glass of wine or suchlike. See reverse of flyer/ticket for details, offer applies in participating restaurants only. Tickets cheaper before 17.00. Concessions available to students & the retired. Wheelchair accessible, loop system for hearing-aid users.

Kino Washington St; ☎ 021 427 1571; e kinocinema@indigo.ie; www.kinocinema.net [E3]
Cork's independent arthouse cinema & an important venue during the annual film festival in Oct. Small & cosy with coffee available. Programmes run from Fri–Thu. Tickets cheaper before 18.00. Concessions available to students & the retired. They occasionally show films that do not have an Irish Cert as they have not been seen by the Irish Censor Board. Membership is required to see these films. Up to 3 tickets can be bought with a membership card.

Triskel Cinematek Triskel Arts Centre, 14a Tobin St; ☎ 021 427 2022; e info@triskelartscentre.com; www.triskelartscentre.com [F3]
Visual arts, comedy, theatre, music, workshops, food — all of these are on offer at some point in the Triskel Arts Centre (see pages 170–1), but it is also an important cinema venue. Specialising in arthouse & foreign films, it is run on a membership system & members must be over 18 years of age. This is because many of the films shown are uncertified. Screenings take place at various times of the day, but no one film is shown for very long, usually just a few days, so if it's something you really want to see, I recommend booking in advance. Concessions available to OAPs, students & the unemployed. Members can buy 2 guest tickets in addition to their own.

LIVE MUSIC VENUES

Lots of places have live music nights; the following are the main venues.

♫ **Beale Street Blues Bar** 3 Union Quay; ☎ 021 496 4900; e annetspijker@eircom.net; www.bealestreetcork.com [H3]
Named after Beale Street in Memphis, the Beale Street Blues Bar (see page 129) is a pub with a clear identity – bringer of high-quality live blues & rock to the discerning Cork public. Regular gigs feature a range of international blues musicians & there are even afternoon sessions to accommodate the younger fans.

♫ **Cork Opera House** Emmet Pl; ☎ 021 427 0022; e info@corkoperahouse.ie; www.corkoperahouse.ie [F2]
Gigs, operas, festival events. See also pages 35, 134–5, 158, 179–80.

♫ **Crane Lane Theatre** Phoenix St; ☎ 021 427 8487 [G3]
This pub (see pages 123 & 131) has a variety of live mid-week entertainment on offer, including jazz, traditional Irish music, cabaret as well as various well-known local & international acts.

♫ **An Crúiscín Lán** 18–20 Douglas St; ☎ 021 431 6428 [H4]
Singer-songwriter nights as well as various international artists. (See page 128.)

♫ **Cyprus Avenue** Caroline St; www.cyprusavenue.ie [G3]
Located above the Old Oak (see page 123) where you can usually buy tickets, this is a key venue for live music, Irish & international.

🎵 **The Half Moon Club** Back of the Opera House, Half Moon St; ☎ 021 427 0022 [F2]
Not as active as it used to be on the live music circuit but there are still gigs here from time to time.

🎵 **The Savoy** Patrick St; ☎ 021 425 1419; www.savoycork.com [G2]
A popular nightclub (see pages 132–3), it's also one of the best places to catch both Irish & international acts. Tickets should be bought well in advance.

🎵 **An Spailpín Fánach** 27–9 South Main St; ☎ 021 427 7949 [E3]
Live traditional music most nights. See page 127.

🎵 **The Triskel Arts Centre** 14a Tobin St; ☎ 021 427 2022; e info@triskelartscentre.com; www.triskelartscentre.com [F3]
An intimate, seated venue & an important location during the internationally renowned Guinness Jazz Festival every Oct, a night of music at the Triskel always promises to be a rewarding one: their gigs are invariably booked out. Featuring a diverse range of artists, from local singer-songwriters to German electro-pop outfits to groundbreaking French multi-instrumentalists – if you want a surprise night out, I suggest going to a gig, any gig – in the Triskel, preferably someone's you've never heard of. It will be all the more memorable for being unexpected & unpredictable. Concessions available to OAPs, students & the unemployed. See also pages 170–1.

8 Shopping

The great thing about shopping in Cork is that everything is within comfortable walking distance of everything else. All the shops are concentrated around Patrick Street and Oliver Plunkett Street and the various little streets running off them. Saturdays can be pretty hectic with crowds of people thronging the streets regardless of the weather. There is late opening on Friday nights with many shops open till 20.00 or 21.00. This is a good time to go clothes shopping as there are rarely queues for the changing rooms at this hour! Most of the high-street stores open on Sundays too (usually 12.00–18.00), but a lot of smaller shops don't.

There is a market every Saturday on Cornmarket Street. A rather hit-and-miss affair, there are occasionally some interesting stalls. Shoes, plants, woolly jumpers, secondhand CDs, homemade cheeses – it's quite a mixed bag.

North Main Street is a busy shopping street too, especially on a Saturday. There are no high-street stores here; most of them are independently owned and there are a lot of discount shops.

The Paul Street area is what could be considered Cork's boho district with lots of little quirky shops and cafés. This is where all the teen Goths (the Paul Rats) like to congregate on a Saturday.

At the time of writing Cork's shopping district was going through considerable change. Many of the small independent shops were being edged out by British and American chains and there were plans for at least two or three new shopping centres all within striking distance of each other within the city centre. The hope is that this will bring shoppers back into the city centre as many have turned to peripheral shopping centres (such as Mahon Point and Blackpool) where, more often than not, there is free parking. Obviously rejuvenation of the city centre is a good thing but I think Cork is in danger of losing a lot of its character as locally owned businesses are forced to close down due to increasingly high rents.

There is a government levy of 15c on plastic bags. The charge was introduced in 2002 in an effort to encourage people to reuse bags. Many shops now use paper bags, on which there is no charge. Revenue generated by the levy is put towards various environmental projects.

ANTIQUES

Savoy Antiques and Jewellery Bowling Green St; ☎ 021 427 7489 [G2] Specialising in antique jewellery. There is nothing else on this street so it's impossible to miss this small shop.

ALTERNATIVE

Dervish and Lotus Cornmarket St; ☎ 021 427 8243; e hungryelephant@eircom.net [E2] Essentially two shops in one, they specialise in gifts, healthcare & holistic treatments. Crystals, ethnic jewellery, soft furnishings &

esoteric books. Dervish, on the ground floor, has a large array of unusual bits & pieces. Lotus, on the first floor, sells Fairtrade gifts (eg: Himalayan crystal salts) & is also a therapy centre (Indian head massage, shiatsu, iridology, etc). If you are interested in having your tarot cards read, or finding out about any kind of mind, body, spirit classes or groups this is the best place to contact. Walnut Books are also based in here (see *Speciality books*, page 144).

Fuchsia Aromatherapy 10 Cornmarket St; ☎ 021 427 9106 [F2] Supplier of essential oils, carrier oils, moisturising creams & lotions, aromatherapy accessories. Vouchers available for treatments in holistic deep-tissue massage, reflexology, aromatherapy, etc.

The Mulberry Tree 5 Kyle St; ☎/f 021 427 4844; e info@themulberrytree.ie; www.themulberrytree.ie [E2] Specialising in personalised handmade wedding stationery, they also sell crystals, jewellery, wedding albums & gemstone gifts. They also provide a wedding rental service (candelabra etc).

Priya 15 French Church St; ☎ 021 490 5986; www.priyatherapy.com [F2] This little shop specialises in luxury natural skincare products. They also sell gift products like oil burners & candles. Upstairs they have treatment rooms where you can have massages & facials, Ayurvedic treatments, hot stone therapy, body scrubs & reiki.

The Red Admiral 4 Fenn's Quay, Sheares St; ☎ 021 427 9121; e admin@redadmiral.ie; www.redadmiral.ie [E3] An acupuncture, reflexology & Chinese herbal medicine clinic. They also sell nutritional supplements.

Utopianation 86 Barrack St; ☎ 021 484 7111; www.utopianation.com [E4] 'Freedom of lifestyle' is the concept Utopianation are peddling. Fairtrade jewellery, locally designed clothes, art, music, tattoo & body piercing paraphernalia, & of course indoor gardening equipment.

BOOKSHOPS

NEW BOOKS

Eason 113–15 Patrick St; ✆ 021 427 0477 [G2] Bookshop specialising in stationery, regional & foreign newspapers, magazines & art supplies. Small café on second floor.

Liam Ruiséal's 49–50 Oliver Plunkett St; ✆ 021 427 0981 [G3] Specialising in school books, they also have a large selection of local interest books.

Waterstone's 69 Patrick St; ✆ 021 427 6522; f 021 427 6253; www.waterstones.com [F3] Largest range of books in the city.

SECONDHAND BOOKS

Connolly's Rory Gallagher Pl; ✆ 021 427 5366 [F2] Overflowing with books, Connolly's has a great selection of secondhand Irish books, fiction & non-fiction, as well as all the usual categories.

Good Yarns Unit 7 Market Parade, St Patrick's St; ✆ 021 427 0968 [F3] Not many people know about this tiny secondhand shop but it's a great place for recent fiction titles at very reasonable prices. A good place to sell any books taking up too much room in your limited luggage space.

Vibes and Scribes 3 Bridge St; ✆ 021 450 5370 [G2] Something of a secondhand department store, Vibes & Scribes have three floors worth of new, remaindered & secondhand books & music. Movie rental also — arthouse videos & DVDs. They now have a second branch close by on Lavitt's Quay.

SPECIALITY BOOKS

Dervish 50 Cornmarket St; ✆ 021 427 8243 [E2] As well as crystals & soft furnishings, this small shop also sells a range of mind, body, spirit. Walnut Books (see next page) also have an outlet here.

Other Realms Paul St Shopping Centre (upstairs); ✆ 021 422 2224; www.otherrealms.com [F2] Specialists in sci-fi, fantasy & horror, videos & DVDs as well as books. They also stock a large range of graphic novels, figures & animé, war gaming & role-playing products as well as all the relevant merchandise — swords, dragons, posters, etc. They also have a café (popular with teenagers) & internet/computer gaming access.

Mainly Murder Bookstore 2a Paul St; ✆ 021 427 2413 [F2] A fairly self-explanatory name really, this small shop stocks an extensive range of crime novels & thrillers, both Irish & international, new & secondhand.

Veritas Carey's Lane; ✆ 021 425 1255; f 021 427 9165; e corkshop@veritas.ie; www.veritas.ie [F2] Religious bookshop.

Walnut Books The Crystal Connection, 50 Cornmarket St; ✆ 021 427 8243; www.walnutbooks.com [E2] Books on sustainability. They have a small outlet on the ground floor in Dervish (see previous page). If you're interested in permaculture, natural building, organic gardening, renewable energy, eco-village design & related topics, this is the place to lay your hands on some information. Their website is excellent.

CLOTHES AND FASHION

Patrick St A-Wear, Brown Thomas, Dorothy Perkins, FCUK, Fitzgerald Menswear, Gentleman's Quarters, Mango, Moderne (teen fashions & jeans), Monsoon, Oasis, Penneys (Primark), Quills (men & women, trendy & respectable), River Island, Schuh, Vero Moda, Warehouse

Merchant's Quay (including concessions in **Debenhams**) Bay Trading, Dorothy Perkins, Faith (shoes), Gasoline (designer jeans), Jane Norman, Liz Claiborne, Miss Selfridge, Morgan, Next, Principles, Pull & Bear (casual clothing & accessories for young people), Top Shop, Top Man

Oliver Plunkett St Benetton, Betty Barclay, Carl Scarpa (shoes), Honey (stockists of Lipsy & French Kitty), Saville Menswear

Princes St Luca (beautiful shoes & bags), Ann Summers (lingerie, hen party paraphernalia), Korkys (trendy shoes)

French Church St Beth (designer clothing, very expensive), DV8 (funky shoes), Le Soul (funky trainers), Monica John (upmarket designer fashion), Store (urban streetwear)

Grand Parade Timberland (outdoor clothing & footwear)

Washington St Prime Time (funky streetwear & skatewear)

Castle St Woodstock (stockists of Birkenstock)

North Main St Miss Diesel (trendy teen/young adult fashions)

Bridge St Incide (surf 'n' skate gear)

Drawbridge St (between Emmet Pl & Patrick St) Samui (designer glamour)

Maylor St Lisboa (shoes & jewellery, lesser known designers)

Winthrop Arcade Designer Fusion (local designers, beautiful clothes)

ALTERNATIVE/SECONDHAND

Moonshine Unit 8, Paul St Shopping Centre; ☎ 021 450 9247 [F2] Ethnic & Gothic clothing & accessories. Body jewellery & People's Republic of Cork T-shirts.

Utopianation 86 Barrack St; ☎ 021 484 7111; www.utopianation.com [E4] Fairtrade clothes & locally designed items.

Bradleys 81–2 North Main St; ☎ 021 427 0845; e micreedon@eircom.net; www.bradleywines.com [E2]
A small supermarket, a delicatessen, take-away hot beverages — all at reasonable prices. They also have an off-licence at the back.

Bubble Brothers English Market; ☎ 021 425 4641 [F3] Friendly service & expert advice on fine wines, champagne & cigars. They cater for weddings, corporate functions & gifts.

The Chocolate Shop English Market; ☎/f 021 425 4448; e info@chocolate.ie; www.chocolate.ie [F3] Being a chocaholic I took my chocolate shop research very seriously & strayed from my regular, The Chocolate Shop (formerly known as Le Mannekin P), for a while in order to give the others a fair chance. But only for a short while. In fairness, they're all great, but that corner counter in the English Market is my firm favourite. As well as high-cocoa-content bars, sugar-free bars for diabetics, seasonal novelties & chilli-chocolate bars, they have all the usual glamorous presentation boxes & ribbons but they also have a more casual side, encouraging you to browse their multitudinous handmade Belgian chocs before popping your selection in a paper bag for immediate greedy consumption. They also sell ice cream during the summer & sometimes take-away hot chocolate during the winter. Try their white-chocolate champagne truffle.

Carry Out 22 Washington St; ☎ 021 427 6314 [D3] General off-licence, selling beers, wines & spirits.

The English Market Grand Parade [F3] This is the best place to go for gourmet food. Lots of organic fruit & veg stalls, cheeses, olives, cured meats, chocolate, wines. And all under one roof.

Heaven's Cakes English Market [F3] Just when you think you can't handle any more lamb shanks or sheep's stomach, up pops a little display unit with the most luxuriant cakes imaginable. Whether you like them fruity & colourful or creamy & gooey, Heaven's Cakes will almost certainly have some sort of a tartlet that will catch your eye. The cakes here are not cheap, but once you have tasted them you'll be practically throwing blank cheques at them.

O'Donovan's 48 Oliver Punkett St; ☎ 021 427 7626; e info@odonovansofflicence.com [G3] Off-licence, selling beers, spirits & wines. They often have special-price deals.

Petits Fours 27 Washington St West; ☎ 021 480 6530; www.petitsfours.ie [E3] Authentic French patisserie with all homemade pastries. They also stock imported French produce such as biscuits, pate, handmade chocolates, traditional pink lemonade, Fairtrade hampers, etc. Try the mendiants: chocolate Grenache with mixed nuts — divine.

The Wine Buff 4 Washington St West; ☎/f 021 425 1668; e barry@thewinebuff.com; www.thewinebuff.com [E3] Stepping into the bijou Wine Buff, located in what used to be an old post office, is like stepping into a world entirely unlike the one you actually inhabit. Leave the grime & the traffic & the busy schedule behind & allow yourself the treat of soaking up some old-world ambience as you select for yourself a good wine at a reasonable price. This, after all, is the Wine Buff's raison d'être. Run by a small but expert group of wine enthusiasts who take the pain & guesswork out of hunting for the perfect bottle of wine. Specialising in French wines, but with a growing portfolio of wines from Italy, Spain & Germany, they deal directly with small, family-owned vineyards themselves, thus keeping the prices down. The wines are chemical-free so hangovers are minimal. With free tastings as well as curious little aids to help you determine the bouquet, the Wine Buff is always an interesting visit. Staff are friendly & knowledgeable & let you take your time. The Wine Buff also runs wine appreciation courses & wine tasting evenings, they cater for wedding receptions & corporate events & sell a range of personalised hampers, wine accessories & personalised corporate gifts. If you've nothing more than a tenner to spend on a bottle of wine, trust me, this is the place to spend it. *Open Tue–Sat 10.30–20.00. Tastings Thu–Sat 12.00–19.30.*

HEALTH FOOD

Here's Health 51 Patrick St; ☎ 021 427 8101 [F3] Allergy-testing specialists, they sell wholefoods & natural remedies. They also carry a small selection of health books & relaxation CDs.

Natural Foods 26 Paul St; ☎ 021 427 7244 [F2] A small friendly shop selling health snacks, dietary supplements, tasty pizza slices, various organic spelt-bread, & herb & seed-bread sandwiches.

Quay Co-op 24 Sullivan's Quay; ☎ 021 431 7753; e quaycoop@eircom.net; www.quaycoop.com [F3] Wholefood shop & bakery, with a vegetarian café spread over the top 2 floors (see pages 111–12), the Quay Co-op provide an extensive range of organic fruit & vegetables, health snacks, herbs & spices, dietary supplements, cosmetics & eco-friendly cleaning products. The bakery produces organic breads, bagels, rolls & cakes for special dietary needs. All are freshly baked daily.

See also *Supermarkets*, pages 151–3.

GIFTS

Fellini 4 Carey's La; ☎ 021 427 6083 [F2] The Fellini 'way of life' is an expensive one. A gift shop, but also a sort of gallery with a random selection of art, jewellery, clothes & designer knick-knacks. Beautiful things but not cheap. Don't break anything.

House of Gifts 11 Princes St; ☎ 021 427 5882 [F3] Traditional Irish gifts, lots of Waterford Crystal, Celtic jewellery, Aran jumpers, etc.

Joyce's 30 Princes St; ☎ 021 427 1143 [G3] Some beautiful children's toys & art supplies.

Pinocchio's 2 Paul St; ☎ 021 427 1771 [F2] Beautiful wooden toys for children; puzzles & games for adults.

Yesterday's 2 Carey's La; ☎ 021 427 6105 [F2] A quaint little shop specialising in antique-style gifts.

HOME FURNISHINGS

Brown Thomas 18–21 Patrick St; ↘ 021 480 5555; www.brownthomas.com [G2] High-quality soft furnishings & designer kitchenware & glassware; everything from Stephen Pearce to Jamie Oliver.
Marble and Lemon 2 Emmet Pl; ↘ 021 427 1877 [F2] Contemporary & traditional furniture. Designer glassware. Pottery & lighting accessories.
Meadows and Byrne Homestores 22 Academy St; ↘ 021 427 2324 [F2] Specialising in designer pottery, they have 3 floors of home furnishings.

JEWELLERY

Azure 8 Carey's La [F2] Some lovely pieces & some very pretty bags.
Equinox 12 Carey's La; ↘ 021 427 8949 [F2] Lavish pieces with matching extravagant prices.
IMB Design 10a Paul St; ↘ 021 425 1800 [F2] Very pretty jewellery; subtle pieces, often with Celtic designs.

MUSIC

ALTERNATIVE MUSIC

Plugd 4 Washington St; ↘ 021 427 6300; e plugd@eircom.net [F3] New & secondhand alternative music. They also carry the difficult-to-come-by music magazine *Foggy Notions*, as well as the ever-popular People's Republic of Cork T-shirts. They also act as a ticket outlet for gigs.
The Vinyl Room 79 Grand Parade (above Singer Sewing Centre); ↘ 021 427 3379 [F3] The entrance to this

small specialist shop is from Washington St. A popular place with DJs, they sell all kinds of house, hip-hop, drum 'n' bass, techno, funk & disco — all on vinyl.

MAINSTREAM MUSIC

HMV 81 Patrick St; ℡ 021 427 0447 [F3] Records, CDs, cassettes, books, accessories, DVDs.

Virgin Megastore Queens Old Castle, Grand Parade; ℡ 021 427 9299 [F3] Records, CDs, cassettes, books, accessories, DVDs. Probably the largest range in the city.

TRADITIONAL MUSIC

The Living Tradition 45a MacCurtain St; ℡ 021 450 2564; e info@thelivingtradition.com; www.thelivingtradition.com [G2] Well-established music shop, specialising in trad, ethnic & world music, selling CDs, cassettes, instruments & music books.

Opus II 131 Oliver Plunkett St; ℡ 021 4279611 [G3] Specialising in sheet music.

Pro Musica Jem Music Hse, 20 Oliver Plunkett St; ℡ 021 427 1659 [G3] Selling instruments & accessories, specialising in sheet music.

OUTDOOR SHOPS

The Great Outdoors 23 Paul St; ℡ 021 427 6382 [F2] Skiing, hillwalking & backpacking equipment.

Mahers Outdoors 7–8 Parnell Pl; ℡ 021 427 9233 [H2] Mountaineering & hillwalking clothing & equipment.

The Matthews Centre Academy St; ℡ 021 427 7633 [F2] Hillwalking, skiing, sailing gear. They also have a small trendy shop called Tubes selling skate/surf gear. The address is Academy St but the shop is technically on Half Moon St (at the back of the Crawford Gallery).

Out and About 24A Paul St; ℡ 021 427 1432 [F2] Camping gear.

SUPERMARKETS/DEPARTMENT STORES/SHOPPING CENTRES

Brown Thomas 18–21 Patrick St; ℡ 021 480 5555; www.brownthomas.com [G2] Brown Thomas is Ireland's upmarket department store. Expect all the usual designer names (Irish & international) & designer prices. Three floors of fashion, make-up, perfume & home furnishings. *Open Mon & Wed 09.00–19.00, Tue 09.30–19.00, Thu 09.00–20.00, Fri 09.00–21.00, Sat 09.00–19.30, Sun 12.00–18.00.*

Debenhams 12–17 Patrick St; ℡ 021 427 7727 or 1890 564008; www.roches-stores.ie [G2] Formerly Roches Stores (a mid-range Irish department store) Debenhams had just taken over at the time of writing so opening hours may have changed in the meantime. The store contains outlets for such high-street fashion chains as Jane Norman, Next, Top Shop, Top Man, Miss Selfridge, Pull & Bear, Faith, Morgan, Bay Trading, Principles, Liz Claiborne & Dorothy Perkins. It also has a car park (see page 69). *Open Mon–Wed 09.00–18.00, Thu & Fri 09.00–21.00 (supermarket from 08.00), Sat 09.00–18.00 (supermarket from 08.00), Sun 12.00–18.00.*

Dunnes Stores 105 Patrick St; ℡ 021 427 0705, Merchant's Quay Shopping Centre; ℡ 021 427 4200, North Main St Shopping Centre; ℡ 021 427 6660; www.dunnes-stores.ie. An Irish chain, Dunnes sells food & clothes as well as some home furnishings. Their own-brand products are usually very cheap. The Patrick St branch is a supermarket with a sale shop upstairs selling discounted clothing & home furnishings. Merchant's Quay is just clothing & North Main Street is a supermarket & clothing store. *Patrick St groceries branch open Mon–Wed 08.00–21.00, Thu & Fri 08.00–22.00, Sat 08.00–20.00, Sun 11.00–20.00. Patrick St textiles open Mon–Wed, Sat 09.00–18.30, Thu & Fri 09.00–21.00, closed Sun. Merchant's Quay branch open Mon–Wed 09.00–18.30,*

Thu & Fri 09.00–21.00, Sat 09.00–18.30, Sun 12.00–18.00. North Main St branch open Mon–Wed 09.00–18.30, Thu & Fri 09.00–21.00, Sat 09.00–18.00, closed Sun.

Marks & Spencer 6–8 Patrick St; ✆ 021 427 5555; www.marksandspencer.com [G2] A mid-range if slightly more expensive department store with men's & ladies' fashions, some home furnishings, a small but popular own-brand supermarket & an off-licence. *Open Mon–Thu 09.00–18.30, Fri 09.00–21.00, Sat 09.00–18.30, Sun 12.00–18.00.*

Merchant's Quay Shopping Centre 1–5 St Patrick's St; ✆ 021 427 5466 [G2] At the time of writing, this was the biggest shopping centre in Cork city, but there were plans afoot for more shopping centres. It has two levels & incorporates Marks & Spencer, Debenhams & Dunnes Stores (clothes only) as well as Boots Pharmacy (also found on Patrick St), Laura Ashley & several other smaller shops including clothes shops, jewellers, health shops, cafés & many more. *Open Mon–Thu 09.00–18.00, Fri 09.00–21.00, Sat 09.00–18.00, Sun 14.00–18.00.*

North Main St Shopping Centre North Main St; ✆ 021 427 0262 [E2] A small shopping centre based around Dunnes (supermarket & clothes shop). It also has a car park (see page 00). *Open Mon–Wed 09.00–18.30, Thu & Fri 09.00–21.00, Sat 09.00–18.00, closed Sun.*

Paul St Shopping Centre Rory Gallagher Pl; ✆ 021 427 1314 [F2] A small shopping centre based around Tesco. Most of the shops in the centre close between 17.30 & 18.00; Tesco has longer opening hours (see below). It also has a car park (see page 69).

Savoy Centre St Patrick's St (opposite Roches Stores) [G2] A small shopping centre including a Champion Sports (sports clothes), Hickeys (fabric), Forgotten Cotton & Gloria Jean's café. *Open Mon–Fri 09.00–17.30, Sat 09.30–17.30, Sun 14.00–18.00.*

Tesco Paul St Shopping Centre, Rory Gallagher Pl; ✆ 021 427 0791, Wilton Shopping Centre; ✆ 021 454 3833; www.tesco.ie. Large supermarkets, both have off-licences. There is a freefone taxi service for customers in the

Paul St branch. *Paul St open Mon–Wed 09.00–20.00, Thu & Fri 09.00–22.00, Sat 08.30–20.00, Sun 12.00–18.00. Wilton open 24hrs, Mon–Fri, but the off-licence has more limited opening hours: Mon–Thu 07.30–23.30, Fri & Sat 07.30–00.30, Sun 12.30–23.00.*

Wilton Shopping Centre Leslie's Cross, Wilton; ☏ 021 454 6944. Has a large 24hr Tesco (see above) as well as a few clothes shops, newsagents, etc. The number 14 bus takes you from the city centre (Patrick St) to the shopping centre, but there's nothing there that you can't get in town. The 24hr Tesco can be useful, however.

9 Walking Tours

I've devised two separate walking tours: the first is a short meander around the streets in the city centre, the second is a longer and more circuitous ramble around the edge of the city centre – don't worry, it's still within the bounds of the city and is not in any way taxing. The two can easily be combined. I'd suggest starting with the city-centre stroll which will conveniently take you through the English Market (see pages 184–5) where you can stock up on picnic supplies to be later devoured in one of Cork's more scenic spots cleverly incorporated into Walk 2. The walks can probably be completed in less time than I have allowed but they're not designed to be power walks – the more time you take, the more you'll take in. I also recommend that you don't leave it too late before setting off on Walk 2, to make sure you complete it during daylight hours.

WALK 1 – CITY CENTRE *Approx 1 hour*

Start on the north side of **Parnell Bridge** [H3] at the eastern end of South Mall and walk westwards down the Mall. The financial and banking district for 200 years, the Mall was once a busy river channel. In 1801 it was filled in. The first point of interest you encounter is on the right-hand side on the corner of Pembroke Street. The fabric shop with the yellow and blue façade was formerly the **Cork Library Society** [H3]. Next along is the **Imperial Hotel** [G3], designed originally by Thomas Deane (who also designed the Gaol and the University) as commercial buildings. Both William Thackeray and Charles Dickens stayed there. The Imperial is followed directly by a building constructed from red bricks, bricks that originally formed the ballast of a Dutch cargo ship. Note the ground-level archway and steps leading to the first floor further on. The archway would have been the entrance to a boathouse, with steps leading up to the front door. This feature occurs a few times along the Mall as well as on Patrick Street. The first block on the left-hand side of the Mall just opposite is known as **Morrison's Island** [G3], because that's exactly what it once was – an island.

Take a left down Father Mathew Street, and as you are crossing the road have a glance at the **Assembly Rooms** [G3] a little further down on the left-hand side of the Mall, just before Irish and European estate agents. The Assembs, as they are known, are not in use any more; indeed, only the façade is extant. They opened in 1861 as a Protestant Hall in order to hold events beyond the reach of the Catholic Church – boxing matches, operas and the like. Franz Liszt visited here and John McCormack performed here. It was a cinema from 1911 to 1964, after which it was a restaurant for a while. For any film buffs out there, the first film ever to be shown in Cork was shown in the Assembly Rooms, it was in 1896, and the film was *The Cinématographe*. To continue with my random aside, the Everyman Palace Theatre on MacCurtain Street, the Savoy Shopping Centre and nightclub on Patrick Street, and HMV music store, also on Patrick Street, were all built as cinemas originally; they were the Palace, the Savoy and the Pavilion, respectively. And this is to name just a few. Small wonder that Cork has such a popular film festival.

Walking down Father Mathew Street you'll come to a former Scottish Presbyterian church on the left. These days it seems to change identity on a regular basis, and chances are it will be a bar or restaurant of some description. Just beyond it is a bingo hall; many of John B Keane's plays premiered there. At the end of Father Mathew Street on the right, and on the corner of Father Mathew Quay, is **Holy Trinity Church** [G3], the building of which was funded in part by the eponymous Father Mathew. Turn right down Father Mathew Quay and a bit further down on the right is the rather imposing **Bishop's Mills** [G3], a former corn store. Take a right here onto Parliament Street leading back onto South Mall. If you look to the right you'll see the restaurant **Jacob's on the Mall** (see pages 101–2); between 1892 and 1943 this was the site of Turkish baths. If you have the time, pop in for what is bound to be a toothsome repast. Otherwise take a left continuing west down South Mall.

When you reach Grand Parade you'll see the **National Monument** [F3] next to the Nano Nagle Footbridge. This was erected in 1906 in memory of various Irish patriots. Turn right on the Grand Parade (also a former river channel), remaining on the left-hand side for the time being. Frank O'Connor was involved in the setting up of the **Cork City Library** [F3] which appears on the left. Before turning left onto Tuckey Street, have a look at the corner opposite – there's a cannon dating back to

1690, inserted vertically into the ground. This was used as a mooring post for boats before the river was filled in. Walk down Tuckey Street and you'll see the the neo-Tudor façade of the **Beamish and Crawford Brewery** (see also pages 178–9) just opposite on South Main Street. There was a prison here in the 18th century; public executions were common and the heads of the prisoners were mounted on spikes for all to see.

Head back down Tuckey Street onto Grand Parade and turn left. On the left-hand side is the **Peace Park** (see pages 188–9), or Bishop Lucey Park as it is also known. If it is the weekend you might catch Art in the Park (see page 167), an outdoor art sale. The park was opened in 1985 to celebrate the 800th anniversary of Cork's first charter. When you come out of the park turn left and cross the road to the **Old English Market** (see pages 184–5). This food emporium is the best place to stock up on picnic goodies for later. Come out the same way, cross the road again and turn right continuing down the Grand Parade. Cross Washington Street and continue on. On the left you'll see Argos and Virgin Megastore, still often referred to by locals as **Queen's Old Castle** [F3]. This used to be the site of a shopping centre of that name and it is still a popular meeting point. There are always a few people standing outside Virgin looking at their watches or busily texting. The Queen's Old Castle actually marked the site of the King's Castle which flanked the old medieval wall in the 16th century.

Walk straight on towards the Great Outdoors (shop) and take a right onto Paul Street. Head down Paul Street to **Rory Gallagher Place** [F2] where you'll see a sculpture in honour of the rock legend (see box, pages 16–17). Continue straight through the square towards the **Crawford Municipal Art Gallery** (see pages 167–8). Keep to the right of the gallery until you come to the entrance. The Crawford runs a continuing programme of temporary Irish and international exhibitions. The building itself is the former Custom House. Just beyond the Crawford on the left is the **Opera House** (see pages 134–5). The back of the building is a bit of an eyesore, but the front is modern and can look good at night. Look across the river at the red-brick building known locally as the **Doll's House** [F2]. This was the 2005 Capital of Culture headquarters.

Take a right on Lavitt's Quay which will take you to the top of **Patrick Street**, known here as Pana. A wide, meandering street, it is easy to imagine boats making their way down the former river. You'll see a statue of Father Theobald Mathew in the middle of the road. Unveiled in 1864, it commemorates the life of a Kilkenny man who dedicated his life to helping the poor and uneducated of Cork city. Father Mathew believed that alcohol was one of the root causes of the abject poverty he saw all around him. He founded the Total Abstinence Society on Cove Street in 1838 in an attempt to help people to help themselves. His temperance crusade helped thousands and the street off Sullivan's Quay where people queued to take the abstinence pledge was renamed Sober Lane. Just around the corner from Sober Lane is a pub of the same name; God only knows what he would make of that.

Much of the street was burned down in 1920 during the War of Independence and had to be rebuilt. In recent times Barcelona architect Beth Galí designed the new-look Patrick Street and work started on Cork's main thoroughfare in 2003.

Modern fixtures and a more pedestrian-friendly street make wandering through the city centre all the more pleasant. Keep an eye, or ear, out for a famous Cork institution, the **Echo Boys**. The familiar cry of these street vendors selling the evening daily (it hits the streets at 14.00) can be heard all along the street.

WALK 2 – CIRCLING THE CITY CENTRE *Approx 2–3 hours*

Start at the bus station on **Parnell Place**. Facing the river, turn right. Cross the road and continue down Anderson's Quay on the same side of the river. Go past Jury's Inn and cross the road at the lights heading straight on into the old **Bonded Warehouses** [J2] which are next to the Cork Harbour Comissioners. Goods on which excise had not yet been paid (like alcohol and tobacco) were kept in the warehouses overnight and because of the need for security it was and still is quite a sturdy building. Apparently there are no rats in there, even to this day. Now turn around, come back out and turn left.

When you reach Eamonn de Valera Bridge, look across the river and to the right for a view of the **City Hall** [J3]. Turn right and walk along the new pedestrianised boardwalk on Lapp's Quay. Grab a coffee from Gusto or stop for lunch at the Clarion Hotel which will be on your right. Turn left just after

'Echoboy'

158

the Clarion and cross Clontarf Bridge. Before turning right along Terence MacSwiney Quay, glance down Eglinton Street which is straight ahead. At the time of writing, the latest 'tallest building in Ireland' was under construction. There are plans, however, for taller buildings elsewhere in the country, so its reign will be a short one. Once you've crossed the bridge, turn right, passing the City Hall on your left. The original building was burned down by the British Army in 1920; this one was built in the 1930s and officially opened by Eamonn de Valera in 1936. It features busts of Terence MacSwiney and Thomas MacCurtain, both Lord Mayors of Cork, just outside the Terence MacSwiney Quay entrance. Walk on the same side of the road as the City Hall as it is easier to cross at the next intersection from that side.

Continue straight on at the crossroads onto Union Quay, noting as you cross that on Parnell Bridge to your right, the cars drive on the opposite (ie: the right) side of the road. The colourful cluster of pubs on the corner of Union Quay is known as the **Strip**. Charlie's (see page 129) is an early house, serving alcohol from 07.00 except on Sundays, and the Beale Street Blues Bar (see page 129) next door is a live music venue. Next door to that is Taste! The Rory Gallagher Café (see page 112). If it has started raining at this point maybe you should duck into one of the pubs for a pint, or even a hot toddy (whiskey) to ward off the cold you're about to catch from completing this walk in inclement weather.

Continue down the quay passing the **Guinness House** [H3] on your left, followed by the **Cork School of Music** [H3], also on the left, and the **College of Commerce** (Frank O'Connor attended for a while) across the river on the right. The footbridge to the right, linking Union Quay with Morrison's Island, is officially named **Trinity Bridge** [H3] but is often referred to locally as Passover Bridge as it was opened in the 1970s by the Jewish Lord Mayor, Gerald Goldberg. Do not cross the bridge but continue on to the traffic lights. Before you turn right onto George's Quay, look left to see Cork's only **synagogue** [H4] (the blue building just beyond the Lee Garage). This street is known as South Terrace and much of it was owned by the Joyce family. It was to sell property here that James Joyce's father travelled to Cork, a journey that is documented in *A Portrait of the Artist as a Young Man*. Turn right and move up along George's Quay. Look across the water to the right to see **Holy Trinity Church** [G4]. Continue along Sullivan's Quay to Parliament Bridge, and take a left down Mary Street. At the end of Mary Street on the left is **Red Abbey** [G4]. Built in the 13th century, this Augustinian priory is the oldest building in the city. A horse accidentally uncovered vaults underneath the church in the 1800s but these have not yet been excavated.

Take a left at the end of Mary Street onto Douglas Street. Just opposite on the right is the **Nano Nagle Walk** (signposted). Nano was born in Cork in 1718 and was the founder of the Presentation Sisters. Educated in France, she risked imprisonment by setting up schools around Cork city for poor Catholics, who at the time were suffering under British rule. She introduced the Ursuline Sisters to Cork, but their vow of enclosure made her work difficult, so she founded the new order. The Nano Nagle Housing Association on Douglas Street is the site of Nano's first school. It was donated by the Presentation Sisters for social housing. The signposted Nano Nagle Walk takes you around the very serene gardens of the property and finally into the convent cemetery where you will find Nano's grave. Further down Douglas Street on the left is Frank O'Connor's House, now the site of the **Munster Literature Centre** (see also pages 181–4).

Head back down Douglas Street and Mary Street and continue west along Sullivan's Quay as far as the South Gate Bridge which used to be one of the entrances to the old walled city. Look over the bridge to see the **Beamish and Crawford Brewery** (see pages 178–9), formerly a prison and the site of public executions.

Turn left at the bridge and head on up the hill, keeping right at the fork onto Barrack Street. When you reach the Gateway Bar turn right to see **Elizabeth Fort** [E4] just ahead of you, now also the site of a Garda station. The **Gateway** (see page 128) [E4] is the oldest pub in Cork and possibly in Ireland (The Brazen Head in Dublin is another contender for the title). A garrison bar, it was the local watering hole for officers stationed in the Old Barracks (now Prosperity Square, a residential estate behind Centra (shop on the left) and Elizabeth Fort. The Duke of Wellington once slaked his thirst here. At the time of writing Elizabeth Fort was undergoing renovations and not open to the public. When it is open, the visitor can be afforded magnificent views of the city. Have a look at the green postbox on the wall at the entrance of the Fort: it is curious for having both the British and Irish symbols on it.

Turn right down Keyser's Hill, a steep laneway over one thousand years old, and then left onto French Quay and Proby's Quay and continue on up Bishop Street where you'll come across **St Finbarre's Cathedral** (see pages 177–8) on the left.

The site of Cork's beginnings and an impressive structure in its own right, what not many people know is that it was once believed that to be buried in the grounds of the Cathedral meant certain acceptance into heaven, regardless of religion. Therefore many locals took it upon themselves to toss the corpses of their loved ones over the walls at night. There are said to be thousands buried there.

Keep left at the first T-junction, walking past St Finbarre's on the left then cross the road and turn right at the next T-junction. Walk along Gilabbey Street until you come to The Rock (pub) on the left. Turn right onto Connaught Avenue and when you get to the little field look to the right for a good view of the north side of the city. Continue along until you come to the T-junction at Donovan's Road. The **University** (see pages 186–7) is right in front of you and can be accessed by any of the many gates along the road. Ogham stones, the quadrangle, riverside walks, the Honan Chapel, it's a beautiful campus and worth exploring for a while.

University Quad

When you're finished there, leave via the exit at **Gaol Cross** (go through the arch in the north wing of the Quadrangle and down the hill to the left, turning right at the bridge), so named because the Doric portico just to the left at the bridge, and now part of UCC, used to be the façade of the County Gaol. Public executions were also held there. Cross the bridge and when you get to the T-junction look left for a view of the **County Hall** [A4], formerly the tallest building in Ireland. Cross the road, turn left and walk along Western Road until you get to the Western Star (pub) on the left, then take a right down to the crossroads. **Fitzgerald's Park** (see page 187–8) will be on the right. If it's a nice day, this is why you stocked up on picnic goodies. Nice scenery, a playground for the kids and with **Cork Public Museum** also located on the grounds (see pages 174–5), it's a pleasant place to while away a few hours. When you're done there, or are not stopping off there at all, from the crossroads on Mardyke Walk continue straight ahead down Ferry Walk. The Mardyke Sports Complex will be on your left and the park still on your right. At the end of the lane, just to the left is **Daly Bridge** [A3], known locally as the Shaky Bridge. Cross the bridge and head up the steps on to Sunday's Well Road. Make sure it's still bright when leaving the park as negotiating the steps in the dark could be difficult. Turn right on Sunday's Well Road and if you want to visit the **Women's Gaol** (see pages 173–4) take a left on Convent Avenue at Annie's Pub, otherwise continue straight on. There are some lovely houses in the area; it's a nice walk. You'll eventually come to St Vincent's on the right where the UCC music department is located. If the gates to their car park are open there's a fine view of the city to be had from the road, including the three spires of St Finbarre's, which is designed in such a way that you can always see at least two of its spires.

When you get to the fork in the road turn right and head down the hill. Upon reaching the river look across the pedestrian bridge and you'll see a **blue house** [D2] on the corner of Bachelor's Quay. George Boole used to live there. (Ample opportunity here for Boole in the Big Blue House jokes.) Professor of Mathematics in UCC from 1815 to 1864, it was his Boolean algebra that made computer science possible. Don't cross St Vincent's Footbridge however, rather continue along by the river on the same side, passing the **Franciscan Well Brewery** (see pages 125–6) on your left. The brew pub takes its name from the 13th-century Franciscan monastery which was built on the same site. If it's a sunny afternoon, their beer garden is a pleasant and popular spot for a quick pint.

When you reach the next bridge, Griffith Bridge, take a left up Shandon Street and take the second right after the post office. Head up Dominic Street and when you reach the top you'll see the perfectly round **Firkin Crane Theatre** [E1] on your left. Turn left and just ahead of you on your left you'll see the Cork **Butter Museum** and the **Butter Exchange** which now houses the Shandon Craft Centre (see pages 171–2). Beyond the Butter Exchange and on the right is **St Ann's Church** and the famous **Shandon Steeple** (see pages 176–7). You've come this far, you can't not now climb the 100-plus steps in order to ring the bells and admire the spectacular view of the city.

Shandon steeple

This next bit is a little confusing: you may have to abandon my directions altogether and simply ask someone. When you come out of St Ann's turn right and head up to Eason's Avenue, and go straight on towards the **North Cathedral** [E1] which you'll see in front of you. Built in the 1860s, it is the fifth church on that site and contains the Shrine of Blessed Thaddeus McCarthy. A 15th-century bishop to whom miracles were attributed, his relics are now on display in St Colman's Cathedral (see pages 196–7) in Cobh.

At the T-junction, cross the road towards the cathedral and turn right. Go straight down a little hilly laneway turning left at the bottom. Walk past all the colourful houses along Church Avenue, down the steps and then turn right down Cathedral Walk. You'll see The Constellation (pub) on the corner of Watercourse Road. Walk straight past it towards the steps on the hill opposite. Go through the traffic lights and make your way up the steps. Any time you stop for a break here, turn around for some pretty impressive views of the city. Then keep on trudging up the steps, cross the road, more steps, then continue straight up the hill until you get to **Audley Place**. This is the top of Patrick's Hill and I swear the air is thinner up there. Turn right along Audley Place, looking to your right over the field for an amazing view of the entire city at your feet. Continue on down Patrick's Hill, looking straight ahead of you for a great view of Patrick Street and the city centre. When you reach MacCurtain Street on your left, you'll see **Gallagher's Pub** on the corner opposite. Rock legend Rory Gallagher (see pages 16–17) grew up there.

10 Sightseeing

ART GALLERIES

ART IN THE PARK *Peace Park, Grand Parade; open Sat & Sun 10.00–17.00* [F3].
Not exactly a bona fide gallery, but there is art on display and for sale every weekend
in the Peace Park. They have covers for when it rains!

CRAWFORD MUNICIPAL ART GALLERY *Emmet Pl;* \ *021 490 7855;*
e *crawfordinfo@eircom.net; crawfordartgallery.ie; open Mon–Sat 10.00–17.00, closed
Sun; admission free; free guided tours of the permanent collection every Sat at 12.00*
[F2]
Housed in a charming red-brick building that was formerly the Custom House, the
Crawford is central to Cork's cultural lifeblood. Recently renovated to include a
modern gallery for temporary or touring exhibitions, this elegant building also
includes a small shop and café (see page 108).

The Crawford has a fine collection of Irish paintings, Greek and Roman sculpture
casts and multi-media art spanning three centuries, including several by Jack B Yeats.
Their permanent collection comprises over 2,000 works. The Gallery also has a
permanently rotating collection of Louis le Brocquy portraits. Famous for his

stained-glass pieces, Harry Clarke has his own room on the second floor. Some are on display here as are his preparatory watercolour drawings of his Eve of St Agnes window. The sketches are accompanied by excerpts from the Keats poem of the same name.

FENTON GALLERY *5 Wandesford Quay;* ↘ *021 431 5294;* e *nualafenton@eircom.net;* *www.artireland.net; open Tue–Sat 10.30–18.00; admission free* [E3]
Contemporary Irish art in interesting premises – a modern studio and a dark, cave-like space towards the back. The gallery opens into a large sculpture courtyard.

THE LAVIT GALLERY *5 Father Mathew St;* ↘ *021 427 7749;*
e *thelavitgallery@eircom.net; www.lavitgallery.com; open Mon–Sat 10.30–18.00; closed Sun; admission free* [G3]
A small non-profit gallery tucked away down a side street and aimed at benefiting the artists and the viewing public, it is worth visiting for its selection of paintings (many stacked up against each other on the floor), ceramics, sculptures and prints all available for sale at prices starting from €100. Its collection includes works by Pauline Bewick RHA, Sandra Bell and William Crozier HRHA.

LEWIS GLUCKSMAN GALLERY *University College Cork;* ↘ *021 490 1844;*
e *info@glucksman.org; www.glucksman.org; open Tue–Sat 10.00–17.00, Thu 10.00–20.00, Sun 12.00–17.00, closed Mon; admission free* [B4]

One of the most ambitious projects the university has ever undertaken, this stunning award-winning gallery, open since 2004, forms the cultural centre of the campus, linking the educational mission of the university with the cultural life of the region in a dynamic civic space. The 2,300m² building is purpose built, equipped with state-of-the-art facilities and has full access to the rich artistic resources within the university, exhibiting them on both a permanent and rotating basis. Located amongst the trees at the university's main entrance on Western Road, it is the aim of the gallery to provide a range of educational and research activities, lifelong learning programmes and public events to nurture the growth and visibility of art and emerging art forms. Art-lovers can look forward to significant collections being on public display, including the university's modern art collection. There is also a café overlooking the river.

THE PEOPLE'S GALLERY *2 Fenn's Quay; ☎ 021 422 3577; open Tue–Sat 10.00–18.00* [E3]
A small gallery of long standing, the People's Gallery deals mainly with oils on canvas and watercolours. Predominantly Irish artists, not all living, and a few well-known names.

AN TIGH FILÍ *Carroll's Quay; ☎ 021 450 9274; e info@tighfili.com; www.tighfili.com; open Mon–Fri 10.00–17.00, weekends 12.00–17.00 (if there are evening events in the theatre, the gallery will be open); admission free* [F2]
Mid move at the time of writing, An Tigh Filí (which they translate as the poets' house) is a multi-purpose community arts resource centre. Formerly located on

MacCurtain Street, the new premises are on Carroll's Quay, in the Cork Arts Theatre. It aims to promote both new and established writers and artists in a community-friendly environment. It's quite an alternative venue and there's always an exhibition of some kind on display there, whether it be sculpture, painting, performance or cinema.

TRISKEL ARTS CENTRE *14a Tobin St; ↘ 021 427 2022; e info@triskelartscentre.com; www.triskelartscentre.com; open Mon–Sat 09.30–17.30 and for performances; concessions available to OAPs, students and the unemployed (no admission once performance has commenced)* [F3]

Describing themselves as a 'public playground', the Triskel was established in 1979, primarily as a visual arts centre (art and film), but since then the programme has expanded to incorporate music, drama, comedy, literature and education. Their aim is to develop new and challenging work across the arts, forging innovative and experimental ways of thinking about a wider culture. I love the idea that they will work 'anywhere that seems to need art'. The Triskel has the unique potential of a multi-disciplinary venue in stimulating artists to experiment and create while encouraging the public to explore, participate in and enjoy the arts. Their gallery programme is diverse and dynamic, featuring anything from abstract paintings to slide shows. Their music programme (see *Chapter 7*, pages 138–9) is equally innovative while Cinematek (see *Chapter 7*, page 137) specialises in arthouse films. They also provide an interesting selection of courses and workshops, for example pottery, glass painting, introduction to film studies, drama classes. Triskel also have a temporary exhibition space at 21 Lavitt's Quay. They have a nice café at their main centre on Tobin Street (see page 113).

VANGARD GALLERY *Carey's Lane;* ☎ *021 427 8718;* e *info@vangardgallery.com;* *www.vangardgallery.com; open Tue–Fri 10.30–17.30, Sat 11.00–15.00, closed Sun;* *admission free* [F2]
Contemporary Irish artists displayed over two floors. Located in the city centre just between the Amicus and Yesterday's.

MUSEUMS

THE BUTTER EXCHANGE/SHANDON CRAFT CENTRE *Exchange St, Shandon;* ☎ *021 430 0600;* e *info@corkbutter.museum; www.corkbutter.museum; museum open daily Mar–Jun, Sep–Oct 10.00–17.00; Jul–Aug 10.00–18.00, out-of-hours group visits by arrangement, Oct–Apr visits by arrangement; adults €3, students/OAPS €2.50, children over 12 €1.50, under-12s free* [E1]
The Butter Exchange is now home to the Shandon Craft Centre with the **Butter Museum** housed alongside it in the Tony O'Reilly Centre. Back in the 18th century the dairy industry was huge in Cork with butter in particular being exported all over the world. In order to ensure quality control the Committee of Butter Merchants was formed. They had their headquarters in Shandon and it was to the

10

market here that all farmers had to bring their butter in order that it might be inspected by the purpose-hired inspectors. Open round the clock to deal with the large volumes of butter passing through their doors, the market's different inspectors checked the butter rigorously during the different stages. The butter was stored in wooden casks called firkins (hence the name of the nearby perfectly round theatre, the Firkin Crane). Each firkin had a mark on the outside indicating its quality ('first' was excellent, 'sixth' very poor), its weight and of course the word 'Cork'. Severe penalties were imposed on those who tried to fiddle the system in any way. There was even a 'name and shame' scheme whereby local newspapers were given the details of offenders to print for all to behold. Some even went to prison.

As business increased the premises had to be expanded and it was then that the elaborate portico we see today was added. However in the late 19th century a decline in the economy led to a drop in the amount of dairy produce being exported, leading eventually to the Butter Market closing down in 1924. Today a number of shops and workshops known collectively as the Shandon Craft Centre occupy the building. Stained glass, handmade string instruments, ceramics and handmade jewellery are some of the products on display. There is also a small restaurant serving all-day breakfasts and lunches as well as a very pretty little garden café out the back. Leafy and green, it is directly overlooked by the Shandon steeple.

The tour through the Butter Museum allows you to view all the various artefacts involved in the categorising of butter during its 18th-century heyday.

CORK CITY GAOL AND RADIO MUSEUM EXPERIENCE *Convent Av, Sunday's Well;* ✆ *021 430 5022;* e *corkgaol@indigo.ie; www.corkcitygaol.com; open daily Mar–Oct 09.30–18.00, Nov–Feb 10.00–17.00, closed for a few days around Christmas, last admission 1hr before closing; adults €5, students/OAPs €4, children €3, family (2 adults and 3 children) €14, separate admission for each attraction but discount on joint ticket [A2]*

25min walk from the city centre. Walk west along Sunday's Well Rd, take a right at Annie's (pub) on to Convent Av and you'll see it ahead of you. Alternatively get number 8 bus from Patrick St as far as the university, walk north through Fitzgerald's Park and over the Shaky Bridge (officially known as Daly Bridge), turn right onto Sunday's Well Rd, then left up Convent Av.

Completed in 1824, the prison took both men and women until 1878, after which it was female only. It was closed in 1923. When I first visited the women's gaol (as it is more commonly known locally) I was unexpectedly impressed: first by the size of the building and its architectural magnificence (it is suspected by some that the architect, Thomas Deane, made a special effort with the prison in order to secure the commission for the university), and second by its fascinating displays; even the tickets are a novelty. The interior of the prison is magnificently preserved and in some cases reconstructed, and the impact this has on the modern visitor is enhanced by multi-media presentations. Lifelike wax figures and special sound effects give you a fairly realistic impression of incarceration in the 19th century. Eerie in some parts, it is actually very poignant, for the majority of the inmates were there for having done nothing more than steal a loaf of bread. The tour rounds up with an effective audio-visual display in which the plights of the more famous political prisoners such as the writer Frank O'Connor and the Sligo-born Countess Markievicz, the first female parliamentarian in Britain, are counterpointed with those whose only crime was poverty. Watch out for the ghost (I'm serious). You can guide yourself around the gaol using the individual cassette players and headphones supplied on entry.

The Radio Museum Experience, housed upstairs in the former Governor's House, is also worth a look. Dealing with the invention of the radio and its impact on world affairs, it too has its interactive gadgets. Tap out a Morse code signal or watch your voice being transformed into sound waves. Marconi, for obvious reasons, features largely, but there is a tangible Cork connection too – his mother was Annie Jameson, of the Midleton distillery Jamesons, and his first wife was also Irish. There is a fine collection of antique radios on display as well as artefacts such as the microphone used by John F Kennedy during his visit to Ireland. A section of the museum is devoted to 6CK, Cork's first radio station which initially broadcast from the gaol itself. It stayed there only three years, closing down in 1927 and then reopening in 1958 when the studio had transferred to Union Quay. Interestingly, the first station director, Seán Neeson, spent some time imprisoned in the gaol during the Irish Civil War.

CORK PUBLIC MUSEUM *Fitzgerald's Park;* ✆ *021 427 0679;* e *museum@corkcorp.ie; open Mon–Fri 11.00–17.00, Sat 11.00–13.00, 14.15–16.00, open Sun Apr–Sep*

15.00–17.00, closed bank holiday weekends including Sun, and on all public holidays; admission free [B3]

This unassuming museum, which has been preserving the region's rich cultural heritage since 1945, is situated on the town side of Fitzgerald's Park. Located in a Georgian house which was built as a private residence for Charles Beamish in 1845, a modern extension has been added recently. Consisting of temporary and permanent exhibitions, there are relics on display here from as far back as the Stone Age. The display is diverse: the partial skeleton of a giant Irish deer, a literary Cork section, mayoral swords, Bronze Age jewellery, a hand-woven wall-hanging of the 'Walled City of Cork' as well as a scale model of same. Plenty of political memorabilia from the early 20th century also, including clothing, newspaper articles, weapons, photos, ordinary everyday objects, and perhaps their most popular exhibit – a collection of correspondence between Michael Collins and his fiancée, Kitty Kiernan, a collection which provides a rare and touching glimpse into the private life of a revolutionary figure. Detailed maps which light up in different areas at the touch of the relevant button may keep restless children amused (or pack them off to the playground on the other side of the park). The temporary exhibitions are equally diverse; for example, the Rhythm of Light focused on modern Norwegian jewellery. Another exhibition consisted of artwork and plaster maquettes for sculptures that were used in the construction of St Finbarre's Cathedral. It is a small museum but there is a lot in there, including a small riverside café.

CHURCHES/CATHEDRALS

St Ann's Church/Shandon Bells *Corner of Eason's Hill and Bob and Joan's Walk, Shandon;* ☏ *021 450 5906; open daily 09.30–17.00, Sun service 10.00; admission to church is free, church tower and bell-ringing €6 per person, €5 students and OAPs, €12 family (2 adults and 4 children under 15)* [F1]

The easiest way to find it is to walk up Shandon Street and take a right up Dominic Street. You'll see the Firkin Crane, the Butter Exchange and the church all on your left. It's at most a 10min walk from Patrick Street.

The Shandon Steeple on the north side of Cork city is one of the city's most famous and beloved landmarks. Built in 1722, the looming tower atop St Ann's Church is something of a curiosity. The north and east sides of the tower are red sandstone while the south and west are grey limestone. Each side also sports a clock face – known collectively as the Four-Faced Liar because, though by and large accurate, the east and west faces are always a little faster than the north and south faces. Crowning the 40m tower is an 11ft-long salmon-shaped weathervane.

The bells and the view, however, are the church's most famous features, and the ones for which most tourists make the hilly trek to Shandon. There are over 100 steps up to the bell tower where you can see the clock machinery as well as the eight bells which were first installed in 1752. Each bell has its own inscription as does the clock machinery, and on-hand sheet music will assist you in *bell*ting out your pick of their available tunes. Once you have entertained the denizens of Cork city with your mellifluous bell-ringing, you can step onto the parapet outside the bell tower for a truly spectacular view of the city. You will even be awarded with a certificate commemorating the event.

The inside of the church is also worth a quick glance, not least for their collection of remarkably well-preserved old books dating from as far back as 1599. As well as books on medicine and geometry amongst others, there is a King James Bible dating back to 1671 and a collection of John Donne's letters from 1651. The furnishings in the church are quite dark and sombre but if you are lucky enough to arrive while someone is practising on the organ, the atmosphere in there can be quite something.

St Finbarre's
Cathedral

ST FINBARRE'S CATHEDRAL *Sharman Crawford St/Bishop St;* ✆ *021 496 3387;* e *cathedral@cork.anglican.org; www.cathedral.cork.anglican.org; open weekdays Oct–Mar 10.00–17.00 (closed 12.45–14.00), Apr–Sep Mon–Sat 09.30–17.30, Sun 12.30–17.00; services: morning prayer daily 12.00, evening prayer Tue–Fri 16.40 (winter), 17.00 (summer); adults €3, Under 18s and students with ID €1.50; guided tours available, prior booking requested, group rates available on application; donations for restoration appreciated* [E4]
Designed by William Burges and built between 1865 and 1879, the Church of Ireland St Finbarre's Cathedral is impossible to miss. Traditionally, it is the site upon which St

Finbarre first founded his monastery in the 7th century. Floodlit by night, the cathedral has been designed in such a way that no matter what angle you view it from, you can always see at least two of its three spires. Internally stunning; it would be worth visiting while a choir is performing. Information leaflets available in several languages.

OTHER ATTRACTIONS

BEAMISH AND CRAWFORD BREWERY *South Main St;* ✆ *021 491 1100;* e *info@beamish.ie; www.beamish.ie; brewery tour available May–Sep Tue & Thu 10.30 & 12.00; Oct–Apr Thu 11.00; adults €7, students/OAPs: €5, tours limited to 15 people, groups advised to pre-book* [E3]
Located on the site of a former prison, it is impossible to miss the neo-Tudor façade of the Beamish and Crawford Brewery on South Main Street. Beamish is Cork's 'other' stout, and is in direct competition with Murphy's (and of course Guinness, but that's Dublin and so doesn't count). They also produce Beamish Red (an ale) as well as some foreign brews, namely Miller Genuine Draft, Carling Black Label and Foster's. It's Ireland's oldest brewery, and William Beamish and William Crawford first bought it in 1792, but even then it had already been in operation since as far back as 1641. The brewery has been rebuilt and modernised a few times since then to the point that the entire brewing process is now computerised. The company has changed ownership several times down through the years and is now owned by the multi-national brewing group Scottish Courage. Interestingly enough, Guinness

attempted to acquire shares at one point but were unsuccessful. The tour involves a ten-minute video, a personal introduction to the raw materials that go into stout and then a guided tour around the brewery finishing up in the Beamish hospitality suite. Stout consists of water, malted barley, roast barley (which gives it its black colour), hops and yeast. The barley is harvested in Cork, but the hops come predominantly from Kent. It is the petals of the hops that are used – they help add to the aroma as well as stabilising the beer, but they come in pellet form now making them look rather like hamster food, and are incredibly pungent. The malted barley tastes quite good though. Much of the stainless-steel machinery throughout the brewery comes with signs attached outlining exactly what role each plays in the brewing process – useful if you're not paying attention to the guide. The tour finished up with a pint in the hospitality room, and because we were just a small group, we got to pull our own – this is the advantage of taking the tour during the low season if, like me, you have never worked in a pub. I got quite a thrill out of pulling my own pint, although given the early hour I was unable to finish it. The brewery is definitely worth a look, our guide was great and I got the impression that if you wanted more information there would be no problem staying on a bit longer and further practising your bar skills.

CORK OPERA HOUSE *Emmet Pl;* \ *021 427 4308; bookings: 021 427 0022;* e *info@corkoperahouse.ie; www.corkoperahouse.ie; box office open Mon–Sat 09.00–19.0, or 09.00–17.30 on non-performance nights, phone lines open Mon–Sat 09.00–19.00* [F2]

This is the only purpose-built opera house in the country today and when it was originally opened in 1855 as the Athenaeum – a sort of lecture hall – inferior acoustics rendered it thoroughly unsuitable. In 1873 it was remodelled and renamed the Munster Hall but it still wasn't a success. Eventually it was redesigned and reopened as the Cork Opera House in 1877. It proved a popular and successful venue but tragedy struck in 1955 when an electrical fault caused the entire building to go up in flames. In 1963 the foundation stone of the new building was laid, but when the new opera house was finally revealed it met with a lot of criticism. It was an ugly building, completely lacking in the elegant charm of the original. Fortunately the interior was flawless; the design, the décor, the seating arrangements and the intimate atmosphere all met with widespread approval. Thankfully, in 1993 plans were set in motion to beautify the eyesore that was the exterior. The foyer, bar areas and façade were all refurbished so that the Opera House we see today is modern and dynamic and a cultural centre to be proud of. (See also pages 134–5.)

CORK VISION CENTRE/ST PETER'S *North Main St; ☎ 021 427 9925;*
e visioncentre@eircom.net; www.visioncentre.com; open Tue–Sat 10.00–17.00; admission free, daily guided tours around the centre [E2]
Back in 1995 when the sadly neglected and dilapidated St Peter's Church on North Main Street was earmarked for renovation, rumours abounded that this Gothic church was going to be transformed into a very hip and alternative nightclub.

Renovated it certainly was, but a heaving dance emporium was not what the Cork Corporation, its new owners, had in mind.

Today the church is home to the Cork Vision Centre, a forum for learning about Cork's past, present and future. Apart from the lofty white space, the first thing you notice upon entry is the bright, white model city. Incredibly detailed, this 1:500 scale model takes up most of the space downstairs. Multi-media information on the city today is also to hand. There are short films as well as touch-screen computers waiting to provide a plethora of information on every aspect of the city. As well as the tourist information, visiting exhibitions and craft fairs mean that the centre is never standing still. It's always a place worth keeping an eye on.

St Peter's Cork Vision Centre

MUNSTER LITERATURE CENTRE Tigh Litríochta, Frank O'Connor House, 84 Douglas St; \f 021 431 2955; e munsterlit@eircom.net; www.munsterlit.ie; open Mon–Fri 10.30–16.30; admission free [G4]

Located in the house in which Frank O'Connor was born, the Munster Literature Centre is devoted to the promotion and appreciation of quality literary writing, new and old. Their programme includes a series of readings and creative writing masterclasses given by professional writers from all over the world. Twice yearly they publish Southword, a journal which publishes writing from both established and

FRANK O'CONNOR

Better known as Frank O'Connor, Michael O'Donovan was born in 1903 in what is now the premises of the Munster Literature Centre (see pages 181–4) on Douglas Street on the south side of the city. Blarney Street on the north side, however, is where he grew up, and as one of the city's Republican strongholds, it was here that he formed the nationalistic leanings so evident in his writing. Best known for his masterful short stories, it was with the publication of his first collection, *Guests of the Nation*, that he adopted his pseudonym as protection against Ireland's severe censorship laws.

Keen to be involved in the formation of an independent Irish state he became a Republican volunteer during the War of Independence. Although this never amounted to more than delivering secret messages, he was arrested by the Free State forces and interned in Dublin when he was 19.

After his release O'Connor, who was largely self-educated, got a job teaching Irish and eventually a job as a librarian. This latter job was largely thanks to Daniel Corkery, a Cork writer and former teacher of O'Connor's. After he had left school he had kept in touch with Corkery who encouraged him to attend literary meetings held in Corkery's house. It was here he met Seán O'Faoláin, another of Corkery's protégés, who was to become

emerging writers. Works from Munster-based visual artists are also featured. (*Southword* is available in all good bookshops.) They have an index of contemporary a lifelong friend. After working in several libraries around the country, O'Connor was eventually made Cork's first county librarian at the age of 22.

Restless and frustrated by Cork's provincialism he eventually moved to Dublin. The liberal attitudes of the capital suited him better and he soon found himself rubbing shoulders with the likes of W B Yeats. It was around then that *Guests of the Nation* was published, and under the influence of Yeats he became a committee member of the Abbey Theatre, eventually going on to become managing director.

He left the Abbey in 1938 and in the early 1940s joined forces with Seán O'Faoláin and several others to set up *The Bell*, a literary magazine showcasing the writing of such notables as Flann O'Brien, Brendan Behan, Jean-Paul Sartre and Patrick Kavanagh.

During the 1950s he travelled extensively between Ireland, Britain and America. It was in the States that his greatest recognition came, both as a lecturer and a short-story writer, with many of his finest pieces appearing in the *New Yorker*.

In 1962 he received an honorary doctorate from Trinity College Dublin where he lectured until his death in 1966. O'Connor is most admired for his short stories – Yeats compared him to Chekhov – but he also published an autobiography, two novels, five plays and several collections of poetry.

and past writers, both nationally known writers and those that are/were highly regarded within their own area. Their multi-media exhibition documents the life and works of numerous Munster writers, from Frank O'Connor to Dervla Murphy. They also have an extensive audio-visual archive of both Irish and internationally renowned writers reading and performing their own works and sometimes the works of others. Their collection includes the Lannan Foundation Video Library, bringing their current total to over 150 videos. Also in place is a small display of original photos, letters and first editions by Frank O'Connor, Seán O'Faoláin and Daniel Corkery. The Centre also organises the annual Springtime Literature Festival (see page 28) in February and the annual Frank O'Connor International Short Story Festival (see pages 33–4) in autumn. For anyone interested in books, the Munster Literature Centre is a worthwhile trip.

OLD ENGLISH MARKET *Grand Parade (main entrances); open Mon–Sat 08.00–17.45* [F3]
I couldn't decide whether to put the English Market in the shopping section or the sightseeing section, but then I decided that it really is someplace you have to visit regardless of whether or not you are looking to actually spend money. Cold and wet and riotous, the primary aim of this covered market, which dates back to 1610, was always to sell meat and fish, which it still does in abundance, but in later years it has become a much more cosmopolitan affair.

There are entrances to this labyrinthine food Mecca on Grand Parade, Patrick Street, Oliver Plunkett Street and Princes Street, but there is precious little in the way of signage; you may have to stop and ask someone. The best rule of thumb is to walk blindly down one of the many dodgy-looking alleys at the Grand Parade end of Patrick

Street and you will invariably stumble upon it. Originally two separate markets, they were destroyed by a fire in 1980 but then rebuilt as the one market we know today. The English Market is an essential starting point, one-stop-shop even, if you are planning a picnic and want the best in locally sourced and organic produce. Get your bread at the Alternative Bread Company; I recommend their sun-dried tomato and fennel loaves. Pick up some hummus and feta and olives at the Real Olive Co, some chorizo from On the Pig's Back. There are plenty of fruit and veg stalls, as well as Bunalun, an organic shop; Iago, a stall specialising in cheese, fresh pasta, and good coffee; the Chocolate Shop (Le Mannekin P), a Belgian-chocolate stall (see page 146); Mr Bell's, an oriental-food stall, of which there are two within the market, each a fascinating melange of all things Asian – loose basmati, poppadoms, noodles, spices, oils, pastes – everything you need to cook from scratch. Flowers, champagne, books, juices and soups, baguettes, local cheeses (keep an eye out for Hegarty cheddar, traditional cloth-bound, hand-crafted mature cheddar made in nearby Whitechurch), People's Republic of Cork T-shirts and of course all the meat and freshly caught seafood you can stomach. The English Market is also the place to source local specialities tripe and *drisheen* (see pages 98–9), and if you don't fancy cooking them yourself, then pop up to the Farmgate Café (see page 109) located on a balcony above the market stalls, affording great views of the hustle and bustle below. A popular lunch spot where you'll find all the market fare cooked and ready to eat, they also do free coffee top-ups making it the perfect place to while away a few hours with your newspaper. The Farmgate also has noticeboards with lots of information on local events.

UNIVERSITY COLLEGE CORK *Western Road; ☎ 021 490 3000; www.ucc.ie* [B4]

Just a short walk from the main shopping streets, UCC's beautiful campus is well worth a visit for the spectacular trees alone. Giant redwoods and mature oaks and beeches date back to the college's foundation in the 1840s and are dotted all around the campus.

An important room in the ceremonial life of UCC today, the venerable **Aula Maxima** (or Aula Max as it is often abbreviated) in the north wing of the quad functions as an examination hall, a concert hall, a reception area – it's pretty multi-functional really. The east window has a stained-glass panel commemorating George Boole who was professor of mathematics in the 19th century and after whom the university library is also named. Portraits of past presidents of UCC are displayed on the west wall of the hall.

The tiny **Honan Chapel**, which is Hiberno-Romanesque in style, contains 19 stained-glass windows, 11 of which were designed by Harry Clarke. Each window is dedicated to a saint. The mosaic floor depicts the signs of the Zodiac. The chapel is a popular choice with graduates getting married.

The **Crawford Observatory** has very well-preserved instruments, making it unique in Ireland and possibly in Europe. It also contains an equatorially mounted telescope which won a gold medal at the Paris Exhibition in the 1870s. The building itself is unusual for observatories in that it is Gothic in style.

Designed in 1818, the Doric portico of the **County Gaol façade** looms large outside the former entrance. Public executions took place here into the 1860s.

There was a time when the **President's Garden** was surrounded by high walls, but these were demolished in the 1960s and so these beautiful gardens are now available for all to enjoy. Full of colour, they form the backdrop to many graduation and wedding photos.

Not technically a quadrangle with the south side exposed, the **Quad** is nevertheless one of the landmark sites of UCC and comes with all the usual strictly observed collegiate superstition. Walking through the four lawns before graduating, for example, guarantees a fail grade in your final exams. Designed by Thomas Deane, the quad is Tudor Gothic in style, and the buildings are made from limestone.

Located in the north wing, the **stone corridor** houses UCC's famous Ogham stone collection. These stones date from the early Christian era and bear one of the earliest forms of writing. The writing may appear as nothing more than a collection of notches and grooves, but each one has significance.

For the **Lewis Glucksman Gallery** see pages 168–9.

PARKS AND LAKES

FITZGERALD'S PARK *Mardyke Walk; open Oct–Mar 08.30–17.00, Apr & Sep 08.30–20.00, May & Aug 08.30–21.00, Jun & Jul 08.30–22.00, opens at 10.00 Sat, Sun & bank holidays; leave park at ringing of bell* [A3]
All parks are great in the summer; this one is particularly lovely with its colourful flower beds, ample lawns for sprawling on, trees and shrubbery, a pond, a river, a

museum and a well-maintained playground. But it's worth a visit in autumn too, simply for the visceral pleasure of kicking your way through large swathes of crunchy auburn and yellow leaves. The river, the leaves, the crisp air, the clouds, it's actually very romantic.

THE LOUGH *Glasheen*
Walk up Barrack St, turn left on Lough Rd, continue on; the Lough will be on the right.
The Lough ('lake' in Irish) is a small shallow limestone lake located along Lough Road in Glasheen – at most a 15-minute walk from the city centre. Surrounded by grass as well as a footpath and some benches, it is a popular treadmill for joggers as a well as the site of impromptu bouts of football. The swans, however, are one of the main attractions and the little island in the centre is also home to numerous other stocked wildlife – for example, Muscovy duck, Carolina wood duck, European pochard duck to name but a few. There is a donation box, the proceeds of which go towards restocking the lake. The Lough is especially pretty at Christmas when the island in the centre is decorated with fairy lights and carols are piped out all day.

PEACE PARK (BISHOP LUCEY PARK) *Entrances on Grand Parade and South Main St* [F3]
Visitors from warmer climes may be surprised by the amount of bare flesh on display as early as March, but so sun-starved are we, that regardless of how watery the sunlight, or how chilly the air, the merest hint of UV rays has people shedding layers and exposing neon-white limbs in a desperate attempt to get a tan and to

alleviate the gloom of winter. The Peace Park in the city centre is the place where the most instant-gratification sun-absorbing takes place. Throngs of city-workers converge on the tiny park for a convenient lunch hour of sunlight before dashing back to their offices. It's right opposite the English Market so you can stock up on gustatory delights and then either park yourself right in the sunlight or under a tree if you're more of a shade person. There are a few benches, but other than that it's the ground or nothing.

ENTERTAINING THE CHILDREN

CHUCKIE'S ADVENTURE PLAY CENTRE *Doughcloyne Industrial Estate, Sarsfield Rd, Wilton;* ✆ *021 434 4112; open daily 10.00–18.00*
This place is great for slide fanatics with a three-lane mega astra slide, a junior astra slide and a giant spiral slide. They also have a separate toddler area as well as ropes and basketball/football facilities. Like most play centres, they also cater for birthday parties.

CORK CITY LIBRARY *57–61 Grand Parade;* ✆ *021 492 4900;* e *libraries@corkcity.ie; www.corkcitylibraries.ie; open Mon–Sat 10.00–17.30* [F3]
It is worth checking the library website to see what events they have lined up for children. They have regular storytelling sessions as well as colouring clubs and various workshops.

FITZGERALD'S PARK *Mardyke Walk*
Fitzgerald's Park [A3] is, I am reliably informed, a great place to play hide-and-seek. It also has a playground.

FOTA WILDLIFE PARK *Carrigtwohill;* ✆ *021 481 2678;* e *info@fotawildlife.ie; www.fotawildlife.ie*
Lots of space for running around, wildlife, playgrounds, a train and a giant giraffe slide. This is a good family day out. (See pages 200–1 for more information.)

LEISUREPLEX *1 MacCurtain St;* ✆ *021 450 5155; www.leisureplex.ie; open 24hrs a day* [J2]
Like so many buildings in Cork, the Leisureplex is housed in a former cinema, namely the Coliseum. Lots of activities for every age: snooker/pool, tenpin bowling, Q-Zar, video games, disco party nights for 12–15 year olds, the Zoo – a play area with slides, tunnels, and ball pools including a separate area for toddlers.

MARDYKE ARENA (UCC) *Mardyke Walk, Western Rd;* ✆ *021 490 4751;* e *mardykearena@ucc.ie; www.mardykearena.com; open Mon–Fri 07.00–22.30, Sat 09.00–19.00, Sun 10.00–19.00; the children's pool closes at 19.30, Mon–Fri* [A3]
The Mardyke Arena has a wide range of facilities, the two most likely to appeal to children being the children's swimming pool and the climbing wall. The climbing wall was closed temporarily at the time of writing but was scheduled to reopen in January

2007. The Mardyke also does birthday party packages incorporating both the pool and the climbing wall.

THE PLANET ENTERTAINMENT CENTRE *Fitz's Boreen, Old Mallow Rd, Blackpool;* ↘ *021 430 0700; open daily 10.00–midnight.*

Facilities include a health club and bar as well as bowling lanes and pool tables but also an arcade-style video games room for children as well as Cosmo's Fun World which is aimed at the 2–10 age group. Ball pools, bouncy castles, astro-slides, swings, rope climbs and climbing walls. Guaranteed to tire them out. The Centre also caters for children's birthday parties.

TRABOLGAN HOLIDAY VILLAGE *Midleton;* ↘ *021 466 1551;* e *reservations@trabolgan.com; www.trabolgan.com; open daily from mid-Mar to early Nov with the exception of a few midweek dates.*

There are self-catering houses available at Trabolgan for those who want to stay longer but they also welcome day visitors. Facilities include a sub-tropical swimming pool with wave machine and slide, quad bikes, go-karts, archery, abseiling, kayaking, crazy golf, pitch 'n' putt, tennis, basketball, badminton, aeroball (a cross between basketball and volleyball on a trampoline) and numerous other activities. There are bars and a restaurant on site as well as organised activity clubs aimed at different age groups. See website for more information.

11 Beyond the City

HERITAGE CARDS

Dúchas, the Heritage Service, is responsible for many of Ireland's historical sites. If you are going to be in Ireland a while, or are planning on packing a lot of monuments, parks and gardens into your trip, it may be worth your while investing in a Heritage Card. Adults €21, OAPs €16, children/students €8.00, family €55. At the moment Dúchas operates about 80 sites around the country and a Heritage Card entitles you to free admission for a year from the date of purchase. You can purchase the card at any of the participant sites (cash only). Alternatively you can look up their website, print off and complete the application form and either fax or post it to them at the address below. They will send you your Heritage Card within 28 days. If you are in Ireland you can send the form by Freepost. I have highlighted any Heritage Sites in this guide with an **H**.

Heritage Card Officer Visitor Services, Office of Public Works, 6 Upper Ely Place, FREEPOST, Dublin 2; ✆ 00 353 01 647 6587 (from overseas) or Callsave 1850 600 601 (within Ireland); e heritagecard@opw.ie; www.heritageireland.ie. *Open Mon–Fri 10.00–17.00.*

BLARNEY

A mere 8km northwest of the city, the little village of Blarney is always popular with tourists.

BLARNEY CASTLE *Blarney, Co Cork;* ☏ *021 438 5252;* e *info@blarneycastle.ie;* *www.blarneycastle.ie; open Mon–Sat May & Sep 09.00–18.30, Jun–Aug 09.00–19.00, Oct–Apr 09.00–sundown (or 18.00), open Sun summer 09.30–17.30, winter 09.30–sundown (or 17.00), last admission 30mins before closing; adults* €8, *concessions* €6, *children* €2.50, *family (2 adults, 2 children)* €18.50 *(cash only)*
Situated in the heart of Blarney village is the well-known Blarney Castle, or more specifically the well-known Blarney Stone. The Stone famously bestows the gift of the gab on all who kiss it. This idea originates from the garrulous Cormac McCarthy – Lord Blarney – who so infuriated Queen Elizabeth I with his non-committal lip service that she dismissed his waffling as being all blarney. Whatever is said about engaging in the ultimate tourist trap, the castle is set in stunning grounds and it really is worthwhile to have a wander around. Of course, once you are there, you might as well make your way to the top of the castle for that Kodak moment, especially as it is actually kind of thrilling, although if you go there during the summer, try and get there early to avoid the queues. Lying on your back leaning backwards into a hole over a huge drop is not for the faint-hearted. The stone is rather inconveniently set in the wall below the battlements. You lie on your back and lean backwards from the

parapet walk. It's as uncomfortable and scary as it sounds but there is an iron railing to grip onto for dear life. Trying to pucker up as all the blood rushes to your head is easier said than done. Still, like climbing the Eiffel Tower or having Christmas on the beach in Bondi, it's just one of those things you have to do. Caution should be taken when climbing the steps, it can be tricky.

Certain areas of the gardens, in particular the Rock Close, have something of the *Lord of the Rings* about them. Ancient trees and stones steeped in Druidic legend appear all the more mystical with names like the Witch's Kitchen and the Druid's Cave. It is a beautiful setting and a stroll there almost eclipses the thrill of kissing the stone. There is also an arboretum within the grounds which is worth visiting.

During the summer there are also conducted tours of Blarney House which was built in 1874. Considered one of the great houses of Ireland, it has been restored in recent times and has a fine art collection as well as antique furniture and tapestries. Guidebooks are available in English, French and German.

BLARNEY WOOLLEN MILLS *Blarney;* ✆ *021 438 5280;* e *retail@blarney.com; www.blarneywoollenmills.ie; open Mon–Sat 09.30–18.00, Sun 10.00–18.00*
Housed in an authentic woollen mill, this is the place to shop for traditional Irish goods. Cladagh rings, Aran jumpers, Waterford Crystal, Belleek China, Guinness merchandising, Carraig Donn knitwear – it's all here. They offer a mailing service for goods purchased in-store, a clothing alteration service and a special ordering facility. Duty is paid on crystal and china shipped to the USA. Tax is refunded immediately

at the point of purchase for customers from non-EU countries. There is a bureau de change available on the premises.

COBH

Located on Great Island in Cork Harbour, Cobh (pronounced Cove) came to prominence during the 19th century both as an important port and as a health and seaside resort. Victorian holidaymakers came from all over Ireland and Britain to enjoy the clement weather, but with the onset of the Great Famine in 1845 Cobh became better known as an emigration port. A statue of Annie Moore and her two brothers on the waterfront commemorates this – Annie was the first emigrant ever to be processed on Ellis Island. Some 39,000 convicts were also transported to Australia during the 18th and 19th centuries, and they too departed from Cobh.

In 1849 Queen Victoria visited the port and to mark the occasion the town was renamed Queenstown. It remained such until 1921 when the Urban Council changed it back to Cobh. The quality of vessel improved from coffin ship to early steamer to great ocean liner, continuing to transport a steady stream of young Irish people seeking their fortunes in America. These days Cobh is probably best known for its association with steamships – the *Sirius* set sail from Cobh in 1838 and became the first steamship to cross the Atlantic; Cobh was the *Titanic*'s last port of call before it sank in 1912; and when the *Lusitania* was torpedoed in 1915, many of the survivors were brought to Cobh and the victims buried there.

A colourful and pretty little town if you ignore the very industrial Haulbowline Island just across the water, they have band recitals on the promenade during the summer, watersports, golf (see pages 19–21), plenty of pubs and restaurants and it's all just a few train stops away from Cork city. Fota Island (see pages 199–201) is also close by, on the same train route. If there is a problem with the train a bus service will be provided. It's also worth noting that bicycles are not allowed on the Cork–Cobh train service.

COBH TOURIST INFORMATION CENTRE *The Old Yacht Club;* \ *021 481 3301/3612/3892;* e *info@cobhharbourchamber.ie; www.cobhharbourchamber.ie; open Mon–Fri 09.30–17.30, Sat & Sun 13.00–17.00*

COBH MUSEUM *High Rd;* \ *021 481 4240;* e *cobhmuseum@eircom.net; www.cobhmuseum.com; open Apr–Oct Mon–Sat 11.00–13.00, 14.00–17.30, Sun 14.30–17.00.*
Housed in a 19th-century Scots Presbyterian church on the hill overlooking the train station, this small museum commemorates life in Cobh and Great Island during the 18th and 19th centuries. All the original features of the church have been preserved.

ST COLMAN'S CATHEDRAL *Cathedral Place;* \ *021 481 3222; mass: Mon–Fri 08.00 & 10.00, Sat 18.00, Sun 08.00, 10.00, 12.00, 19.00, carillon recitals May–Sep Sun 16.30.*

Towering over the colourful houses on Cobh's waterfront is the imposing French Gothic-style St Colman's Cathedral. The foundation stone was laid in 1868 and the spire was completed in 1915, with 42 bells of the famous 49-bell carillon installed the following year. A further five were added in 1958 and the final two were added in 1998. The largest carillon in Ireland, the bells are tuned to the accuracy of a single vibration and the largest bell alone, named St Colman, weighs 3,440kg. St Colman is the patron saint of the diocese of Cloyne. The enormous Rose Window over the entrance of the cathedral is also spectacularly pretty, but of course can be seen only when you're leaving the church and so is not in danger of distracting you from your prayers. The relics of Blessed Thaddeus McCarthy, who was said to have performed miracles, are also on display here. He was Bishop of Cloyne from 1490 to 1492.

Leaflets (in English, Irish, French, German and Spanish) guiding you around the cathedral's most interesting features are available at the entrance. Donations towards the cost of restoration are appreciated.

THE MOUNT *St Benedict's Priory, Bond St;* \ *021 481 1354*
Go up the hill past St Colman's Cathedral, turn right on Bond St, walk straight ahead; the Mount will be in front of you.
Home of the Benedictine nuns, the Mount is also a meditation centre with a small tea shop, a herb garden and what they call the Bible Garden – a pretty little garden with various plots named after religious figures.

11

THE QUEENSTOWN STORY/COBH HERITAGE CENTRE *Cobh Railway Station;* ↘ *021 481 3591;* e *info@cobhheritage.com; www.cobhheritage.com; open daily May–Oct 09.30–18.00 (last admission 17.00), Nov–Apr 09.30–17.00 (last admission 16.00); adults €6, students/OAPs €5, children €3.00, family (2 adults, 4 children) €16.50*
Upon first entry into the Cobh Heritage Centre you might be fooled into thinking it's just another 'Top of the Morning To Ya' outlet for tourist tat, what with the woolly jumpers and the shamrock, but the main point of the centre is its award-winning Queenstown Story exhibition which is continually updated and very impressive indeed. With plenty of multi-media special effects, the exhibition appeals to both young and old alike and deserves at the very least a good hour to explore. Beginning with the Famine of the 1840s, Irish history is explored from the perspective of Cobh and its status as a port. From the horror of the coffin ships to the tragic glamour of the *Titanic* and the *Lusitania*, the exhibition is moving and worthwhile. I've been several times now and I have no doubt that I'll be back. They also offer a genealogy search service. Their record-finder service costs approximately €25.

SIRIUS ARTS CENTRE *The Old Yacht Club;* ↘ *021 481 3790;* e *cobharts@iol.ie; www.iol.ie/~cobharts; open Wed–Fri 11.00–17.00, Sat–Sun 14.00–17.00*
Formerly the clubhouse of the Royal Cork Yacht Club (oldest yacht club in the world, now operating out of Crosshaven), the Sirius Arts Centre has a small but busy gallery with regular exhibitions and also functions as a live music venue with gigs on the first Thursday of every month at 20.30. Worth keeping an eye out for.

TITANIC TRAIL *Carrignafoy;* ✆ *021 481 5211;* e *info@titanic-trail.com; www.titanic-trail.com*

This fascinating and moving tour explores the history of Cobh with particular emphasis on the town's links with the ill-fated *Titanic*. Duration is approximately 75 minutes and the cost of the ticket includes a glass of Guinness in Jack Doyle's Bar.

Leaves at 11.00 daily from the Commodore Hotel. During June to August there is also a walk at 14.00. Times may vary during the low season (Oct–Mar). €8.50 per person. Children under 12 half price. Minivan tours available on request, duration is approximately 45 minutes and costs €15 per person.

The same company also runs a **Ghost Walk**. It takes place in the evenings for obvious reasons, lasts 45–55 minutes, costs €13.50 per person and includes a cocktail in Pillar's Bar. Suitable for all ages.

FOTA

By car, Fota is 10km east of Cork city. Take the N25 east following signs for Cobh, exit on R624 heading to Cobh; it's a further 2.5km. Alternatively take the Cobh train; Fota is the third stop from Kent station in Cork city (14 mins).

FOTA HOUSE AND GARDENS *Carrigtwohill;* ✆ *021 481 5543;* e *info@fotahouse.com; www.fotahouse.com; open Apr–Sep Mon–Sat 10.00–17.00, Sun & bank holidays 11.00–17.00 (last admission 16.30); Oct–Mar Mon–Sun 11.00–16.00 (last admission*

15.30); adults €5.50, concessions €4.50, children €2.20, family (2 adults, 3 children) €12.50, group rate (15 or more people) €4.50

Fota House is a fine example of Regency-period architecture with impressive neoclassical interiors. Set amidst beautiful gardens and a well-respected arboretum, this stately home offers a very calming visit. You can guide yourself around the house using a series of multi-media programmes located about the premises. There is also a tea room where you can relax when all the sightseeing starts to take its toll.

FOTA WILDLIFE PARK *Carrigtwohill;* ☎ *021 481 2678;* e *info@fotawildlife.ie; www.fotawildlife.ie; open Mon–Sat 10.00–18.00, Sun 11.00–18.00 (last admission 17.00), winter months (early Nov–early Mar) Mon–Sat 10.00–16.30, Sun 11.00–16.30 (last admission 15.30); adults €11.50, concessions €7, family (2 adults, 4 children) €45, groups (20 or more): adults €9.50, concessions €6; car park charges: private vehicles €2; Wildlife Tour Train €1 one way, €2 round trip*

This is a great day out for kids. Fota has over 90 species of wildlife, from all over the world, many of which wander freely around its 70 acres of scenic and tranquil countryside. There are also free playgrounds, a giant giraffe slide, scheduled animal-feeding times, picnic and rest areas, a self-service restaurant and a gift shop. There are also various seasonal children's events throughout the year, Easter Bunny activity days, Hallowe'en activity days, etc. Domestic pets are not allowed in the park, nor are radios or music systems of any kind. Fota Wildlife Park is a non-profit organisation, actively involved in wildlife conservation on a global scale. There are brochures available on request outlining their educational programmes and conservation courses. On a pleasant day, this is a relaxing family day out.

Your ticket also gives you free admission to Fota Arboretum and Gardens.

GOUGANE BARRA FOREST PARK

The source of the River Lee and some 40km from Cork city, there is precious little to do in Gougane Barra but it is incredibly pretty and romantic. St Finbarre is said to have established one of his earliest churches on the tiny island in the middle of the Gougane Barra Lake which is overlooked by the Shehy Mountains. A replica of that monastery was built on the same spot in the 19th century and a small causeway links the holy island to the shore. There are some fine stained-glass windows to be found within, and a large wooden cross supposedly marks the spot of St Finbarre's own cell. You can drive through the park and various nature trails, and picnic areas are signposted.

If driving from the city, head west towards Ballincollig, going out the Carrigrohane Straight (Road) past the County Hall and follow signs for Macroom and Killarney. It's quite a long drive on very bendy roads and it's not always terribly well signposted; you will most likely think that you are lost but persevere, it is worth it. Follow signs for Inchigeela and Ballingeary, two villages en route to the park. It's about 4 or 5km beyond Ballingeary – and, thankfully, it's signposted at that point too!

KINSALE

Popularly referred to as Ireland's gourmet capital, much of Kinsale's charm lies in simply wandering around its pretty streets, inhaling the sea air, trying to decide where you are going to eat. Even the drive there from Cork city is a scenic pleasure, especially in summer when everything is impossibly green. Kinsale is also a great place to shop for high-quality arts and crafts and to engage in activities such as the Rugby Sevens (see page 30). And while Cork city has its jazz festival in October, Kinsale has its own fringe jazz festival (see page 36).

If you are travelling by car from Cork city, follow signs for the airport. When approaching the Airport Road Roundabout, keep an eye out on the right-hand side for a sculpture of Pegasus. The sculpture is in three pieces, and only forms the image of Pegasus at one point as you drive by. Blink and you'll miss it. (It doesn't work in the opposite direction!) Kinsale is about 20km from the airport and the road has a lot of twists and turns. Expect a lot of pedestrians and cyclists so drive with caution, especially if you're not used to driving on the left.

There are over ten buses (number 249) daily (five on a Sunday) from Parnell Place in Cork to Kinsale. The journey takes about 45 minutes.

The town itself is on the site of a monastery founded by St Multose in the 6th century. It was walled by the Normans in the 13th century and established as a significant trading town. Its overseas trade expanded and by the end of the 16th century it was one of the most important towns on the south coast. In September

1601, Spanish forces in support of the Irish rebellion against the English had anchored in Kinsale harbour. They were defeated however in a battle on Christmas Eve. Catholics were subsequently banned from the town, a ban that remained in place for another 100 years.

After the defeat Kinsale continued to develop as a shipbuilding town. In the early 18th century Alexander Selkirk set sail from Kinsale but was shipwrecked on a desert island, thus providing Daniel Defoe with his inspiration for *Robinson Crusoe*.

On 7 May 1915 the *Lusitania*, en route from New York to Liverpool, was torpedoed off the coast of Kinsale by a German U-boat. It took less than 20 minutes for the boat to sink and 1,198 people died. Five of the recovered bodies were brought to Kinsale along with nine survivors.

TOURIST INFORMATION
Kinsale Tourist Information Office Pier Rd; \ 021 477 2234; e kinsaletio@eircom.net
Kinsale Chamber of Tourism Scilly, Kinsale; \ 021 477 4026; e info@kinsale-tourism.ie; www.kinsale.ie

Pick up a copy of the readily available *Kinsale Advertiser* for a diary of events. The website www.kinsale.ie is also a good source of information.

✗ WHERE TO EAT Kinsale has a disproportionate number of restaurants for its size, a lot of them very high quality, a lot of them award-winning and of course, given its coastal aspect, a lot of them specialising in seafood. As I have already said, much of

11

the pleasure to be had from visiting Kinsale is in roaming its streets scanning the menus. There is hardly a dud amongst them so I am not giving the restaurants individual reviews; I'm just going to list a few of the more popular ones.

✘ **The Blue Haven** 3 Pearse St; ☏ 021 477 2209; e info@bluehavenkinsale.com; www.bluehavenkinsale.com. An upmarket hotel, their popular restaurant is more reasonably priced.

✘ **Crackpots – The Ceramic Restaurant** 3 Cork St, Kinsale; ☏ 021 477 2847. Something a bit different, a restaurant with a working pottery. Open evenings from 18.30 & for Sunday lunch. Excellent seafood in pleasantly modern atmosphere, with food served on unusual, locally made ceramic dishes which are also for sale.

✘ **Fishy Fishy Café** The Guardwell (opposite St Multose Church); ☏ 021 477 4453. A critically acclaimed seafood restaurant, they serve only lunch.

✘ **Hoby's** 5 Main St; ☏ 021 477 2200. Modern Irish & European cuisine made from local produce; elegant décor, reasonably priced.

✘ **Max's Wine Bar** 48 Main St; ☏ 021 477 2443. Open during the high season, this is an upmarket little restaurant with a French emphasis.

✘ **Man Friday** Corner of River Rd & High Rd, Scilly; ☏ 021 477 2260; www.man-friday.net. The oldest restaurant in Kinsale. Good food with some terraced seating overlooking the harbour. Book early if you want dinner with a view.

✘ **The Spinnaker** Scilly; ☏ 021 477 2098. Popular award-winning pub-food with a nautical angle.

✘ **Vintage Restaurant** 50 Main St; ☏ 021 477 2502; e info@vintagerestaurant.ie; www.vintagerestaurant.ie. Considered by many to be the best in the town. Expensive but worth it.

ARTISAN SHOPS & GALLERIES

Boland's (Barry's Place); Irish Arts & Crafts (Main St); Quay Food Co (Market Quay); Heather Mountain (Market St); Kinsale Crystal (Market St); Kinsale Silver (Pearse St); Crackpots Pottery & Restaurant (3 Cork St); Keane on Ceramics (Pier Rd); Kinsale Art Gallery (Pier Head); Giles Norman Photographer (Main St); Gallery 23 (1 Chairman's La); Marina Gallery (Pier Rd); Stone Mad Gallery (Newman's Mall).

WHAT TO SEE

Charles Fort *Summercove;* ✆ *021 477 2263;* f *021 477 4347; open daily Mar–Oct 10.00–18.00, Nov–Mar 10.00–17.00 (last admission 45mins before closing);* **H**; *adults €3.50, children/students €1.25, OAPs/groups (20 or more) €2.50, family €8.25.*
By car, take a left just before you arrive in Kinsale from the Cork city side. Well signposted.
One of the finest examples of a 17th-century fortification in Ireland as well as one of the best-preserved star forts in Europe, the fort was primarily constructed as a coastal defence although it was vulnerable to land-based attacks. The design of certain aspects of the fort followed the principles of Sebastien de Vauban, Chief Engineer of Louis XIV and siege-warfare specialist. William Robinson, who designed the Royal Hospital in Kilmainham in Dublin however, is credited with the design of the final product. When the Duke of Ormond, Lord Lieutenant of Ireland, visited the fort in 1681 he named it Charles Fort in honour of King Charles II.

In 1689, James II landed in Kinsale with a view to regaining the throne. In 1690, the Williamites, fresh from victory at the Battle of the Boyne, arrived at Kinsale and attacked both James Fort and Charles Fort. After a gunpowder explosion killed many of the defenders, James Fort surrendered. Charles Fort endured a 13-day siege before it too finally surrendered. Repairs were made soon afterwards with improvements made throughout the 18th century, although Kinsale's importance as a naval and merchant shipping base had been supplanted by Cork Harbour.

The fort continued to be garrisoned throughout the 19th century and was used for training purposes right up until 1921 when the British withdrew with the emergence of the Irish Free State. Much of it was destroyed during the Civil War and it was only in 1971 when it was taken into state care as a National Monument that a programme of repair and conservation got under way.

Worth a visit for the views of Kinsale harbour if nothing else, but there is also plenty to explore as well as some very interesting audio-visual displays both on the defence fort and on life at that time.

Desmond Castle/Wine Museum *Cork St; ✎ 021 477 4855; open daily mid-Apr–Oct 10.00–18.00 (last admission 45mins before closing);* **H**; *adults €2.75, children/students €1.25, OAPs/groups (20 or more) €2.00, family €7.00*
The Earl of Desmond built Desmond Castle in the late 15th or early 16th century and it functioned as the Kinsale Customs House. In 1601 it was occupied by the Spanish who apparently used it as a magazine for gunpowder. Following their defeat the castle reverted to its original function of customs house. During various wars in the 17th and 18th centuries the castle was used for holding European prisoners. In

1747 a fire broke out killing 54 prisoners, the majority of them French sailors, after which it became known as the French Prison. During the American War of Independence it was used for holding captured Americans. During the Great Famine in the 1840s the castle was used as workhouse accommodation. After that it fell into disrepair but since it was declared a National Monument in 1938 it has undergone restoration and part of it has been converted into an International Wine Museum, commemorating the wines produced by the descendants of those exiled Irish leaders who fled the country in the 17th century.

Kinsale Brewing Company *The Glen;* ⟍ *021 470 2124; e info@kinsalebrewing.com; www.kinsalebrewing.com; admission €7, group rates available; tours daily during the summer, by prior arrangement at other times; bar open Mon–Fri from 16.00, Sat & Sun from 14.00*
Purveyors of Kinsale Lager and Cream Stout, as well as Landers Ale and Williams Wheat Beer, the Kinsale Brewing Company also give enjoyable and informative guided tours of their brewery. Taking you through each step of the brewing process, they allow you to see first-hand how they make their beer – from the raw materials to the final product flowing out of their tap. Round it all up by relaxing in the Brewery Bar sampling some of their products.

Autumn Flavours Festival of Fine Food and Fun Unmissable for gourmets and gourmands alike, this is a four-day festival in October promoted by Kinsale's 'new'

11

Good Food Circle (group of reputable restaurants working together) in conjunction with the Kinsale Chamber of Tourism. Many events have tickets available at the door. (See page 37 for more detail.)

MIDLETON

An afternoon can easily be spent taking in the sights just east of the city. Barryscourt Castle in Carrigtwohill is on the way to Midleton, a market town where you will find the Old Midleton Distillery as well as Silverstone Dimensions where you can pick up some beautiful handmade contemporary jewellery.

BARRYSCOURT CASTLE *Carrigtwohill, Co Cork;* ↘ *021 488 2218, 021 488 3864 (winter); open daily Jun–Sep 10.00–18.00, for access during the low season,* ↘ *021 477 2263, access by guided tour only (last admission 45mins before closing); adults €2.10, children/students €1.10, OAPs/groups (20 or more) €1.30, family €5.80. Take the bus (number 260) from Parnell Place to Carrigtwohill; the Castle is signposted from there and is walking distance from the town centre (about 15 mins).*
The Barrys first came to Ireland from Wales in 1180 where they were granted land in Cork. A powerful Norman family, they inter-married with local native Irish families down through the centuries but the main seat of the family was always Barryscourt Castle. In 1581 the family castles fell to David Barry who, upon the death of his father in prison, destroyed the castles rather than see them fall into English hands. However,

when pardoned by Queen Elizabeth I the following year he moved back to Barryscourt, married Ellen Roche and remained thenceforth loyal to the Crown. The castle was attacked and taken in 1645 and by the early 18th century was in the possession of the Coppinger family. In 1987 the Barryscourt Trust was founded with a view to conserving and developing the heritage potential of the castle, especially as the towerhouse was still standing. Dúchas got involved and the towerhouse was restored and reroofed.

Much of the castle we see today is still undergoing restoration and is a prime example of an Irish towerhouse. The guided tour (about 75 mins) through the tower is a must. Trap doors, murder holes and dungeons will appeal to those with an affinity for the macabre, en-suite and family loos (four of you could go at the same time!) will dispel any myths of the Irish being a prudish lot, and there are plenty of replicas throughout the castle to give you an idea of what life would have been like back then. Even the orchard at the back of the castle has been cultivated as it would have been in the 16th century. Our guide was well informed with an obvious genuine enthusiasm for the history of the site and the era.

There is a café selling teas and light lunches next to the castle. In winter it is open only on Sundays.

THE OLD MIDLETON DISTILLERY *Distillery Walk;* ✆ *021 461 3594;* e *bookings@omd.ie; www.jamesonwhiskey.com; open daily Mar–Oct 10.00–18.00 (last tour 16.30), Nov–Feb daily tours at 11.30, 14.30 & 16.00; adults €8.50,* *students/OAPs €7, children €3.95, family (2 adults, 4 children) €22, discounts for booking online.*

Regular buses (number 260) from Cork bus station to Midleton. By car, take the N25 towards Rosslare; Midleton is about 20km from the city.

The Old Midleton Distillery, which dates back to the 18th century, actually closed down in 1975 when a new distillery was opened, but was then reinvented in 1992 as the Jameson Heritage Centre. The original distillery has been carefully restored to its former glory and is indeed an impressive sight. The guided tour begins with a short film after which you are led around the grounds and given an informative lesson on the making of whiskey. The distillery is also home to the largest pot-still in the world, with a capacity of 144,000 litres. Made of copper because it doesn't interact with alcohol, the pot-still is where the distillation occurs. This is especially important as it is the defining factor between Irish whiskey, Scotch and bourbon. Irish whiskey is distilled three times which gives it its purity of taste, Scotch is distilled twice and bourbon just the once. The grain in Scotch is dried using peat, which gives it its smoky flavour, whereas in Ireland the grain is dried with a smokeless fuel. You can put your taste buds to the test if you are one of the first two to shoot your hand in the air when your tour guide asks for volunteers. The chosen two are offered samples of four Irish whiskeys, one Scotch and one bourbon (all mixed with a little water to spare your senses) and given a mini guided tour through the taste sensations by the on-hand expert. You will then be awarded a glass of your favourite for your efforts as well as a certificate announcing your proficiency in whiskey-tasting. Infinitely better than the Pepsi Challenge! If you didn't have the presence of mind to stick your hand in the air, never fear, there'll be a glass of Jameson awaiting you in the bar nonetheless. There's also a traditional restaurant in the centre, and a shop where you can spend just over €50 on a bottle of Jameson Distillery Reserve, a whiskey exclusive to the shop, or in excess of €120 on a bottle of Midleton Very Rare which will be numbered and signed by the head distiller.

SILVERSTONE DIMENSIONS *The Courtyard, 8 Main St;* ↘ *021 463 4758;* e *silverstone@sdyolzari.com; www.sdyolzari.com; open Mon–Sat 10.30–17.30*
One of the best places to pick up some really beautiful and unusual jewellery. Using gold, ebony, silver, pearls, shells and semi-precious stones, goldsmith and sculptor Shmuel Yolzari creates imaginative and often reversible pieces (two-sided pendants!). If you want to go home from your holiday with stunning jewellery that no-one else will have, come to this place.

Not far from Midleton is the small village of **Shanagarry**, home of Ballymaloe House (see pages 78–9 and 117–18) and Stephen Pearce Pottery.

STEPHEN PEARCE POTTERY *Shanagarry;* ↘ *021 464 6807 (original pottery), 021 464 6262 (gallery);* e *info@stephenpearce.com; www.stephenpearce.com; gallery open daily 10.00–18.00, closed Christmas Day*
Located just a few hundred metres from the village of Shanagarry. Follow signs for Midleton and Cloyne from Cork city, continue on, passing Ballymaloe House. From

there follow signs for Ballycotton until you come to Shanagarry village. Once in the village you will see signs for the pottery.

Well-known throughout Ireland and abroad, Stephen Pearce's terracotta and white earthenware is a familiar sight around Cork in particular. The pottery, workshops and gallery are open to the public and there is also a café on-site as well as a large shop should you wish to splash out. The original pottery is located just outside the village and is also open to the public but the main 12,000ft facility is in the village itself in the grounds of Shanagarry Castle.

FCO TRAVEL ADVICE
know before you go
fco.gov.uk/travel

Bradt Travel Guides is a partner to the 'know before you go' campaign, masterminded by the UK Foreign and Commonwealth Office to promote the importance of finding out about a destination before you travel. By combining the up-to-date advice of the FCO with the in-depth knowledge of Bradt authors, you'll ensure that your trip will be as trouble-free as possible.

www.fco.gov.uk/travel

12 Language

The main spoken language in Ireland is English but Irish is protected under Article Eight of the Irish Constitution as the first official language of the state. Despite this, it is considered merely as a treaty language by the EU and is grouped along with other languages such as Flemish and Basque. Petitions are doing the rounds to get a referendum on the subject of making Irish an official EU language.

These days Irish is spoken on a regular basis only in Gaeltacht areas, small rural pockets along the south and west coasts. Most people have a fair smattering of Irish, however, as it is compulsory in schools and for getting into third-level education or the Civil Service. It is also evident on a day-to-day basis in bilingual signposting and in the media. TG4 is the all-Irish television station (with English subtitles) and Raidió na Gaeltachta (94FM) the all-Irish radio channel. Many people argue that Irish is a dying language but Raidió na Gaeltachta has been going strong since 1972 and broadcasts 24 hours a day, with TG4 the fastest-growing television station in the country. People always mysteriously manage to revive their Irish when they're abroad too: fabulous for conversations that need to be kept private! You don't need to be able to speak it to enjoy a holiday here, but recognising a few terms could come in very handy, especially as male and female public toilets are often only identifiable as such by the Irish word on the door.

IRISH

Different areas have different dialects – you might be greeted with blank looks if you used the following expressions and pronunciations in the north but you should be able to make yourself understood in Cork at least!

GREETINGS AND CONVERSATION

Dia dhuit (deea gwit)	Hello
Dia is Muire dhuit (deea smwirra gwit)	Hello (in response to above)
Slán leat (slawn lat)	Goodbye
Oíche mhaith (eeha wah)	Goodnight
Conas atá tú? (kunnas ataw too)	How are you?
Tá mé go maith (taw may g'mah)	I'm good/I am fine
Cad is ainm duit? (kod iss anim dit)	What is your name?
Linda is ainm dom (Linda iss anim dum)	My name is Linda
Is mise Linda (Iss misha Linda)	I am Linda
Go raibh maith agat (gurruv mah agut)	Thank you
Le do thoil (leh du hull)	Please
Tá fáilte romhat (taw fawlcha roat)	You're welcome
Tá/Sea (taw/shah)	Yes
Níl/Ní hea (neel/nee hah)	No

'Yes' and 'no' are tricky ones as it's not usually enough simply to say 'yes' or 'no'; it depends on the question asked. You usually have to respond using the same verb that was in the question. For example, if you were asked: 'Did you see ...?' You would answer: 'I did (not) see.' *Sea* and *ní hea* are usually used when a sentence is followed with *an hea?* (onnah), which loosely translates as: 'Is that the case?' Otherwise just stick with *Tá* and *níl*, people will know what you mean.

An bhfuil Gaeilge/Béarla agat?	Do you speak Irish/English?
(On will gwaylga/bayrla agut)	
Beagáinín (byugawneen)	A little
An dtuigeann tú? (onn diggin too)	Do you understand?
Tuigim/Ní thuigim (tiggim/nee higgim)	I understand/don't understand
Cad as duit? (kod oss dit)	Where are you from?
Is as an ... mé (iss oss on ... may)	I'm from ...
Lá breá álainn is ea é	
(law bra awlinn isha ay)	It's a lovely day
Buíochas le Dia (bweeochas le deea)	Thank God
Sláinte (slawncha)	Cheers

COMMON SIGNS

Leithreas (lehrass)	toilet
Mná/Bean (mnaw/ban)	women/woman

Fir/Fear (firr/farr)	men/man
Dúnta (doonta)	closed
Oscailte (usskillta)	open
Oifig an Phoist (iffig on fwisht)	post office
Go mall (guh moul)	slowly (usually seen in reference to driving)
Gach treo eile (gock tro ella)	all other routes
Siopa/Siopaí (shuppa/shuppee)	shop/shops
An Lár (on lawr)	the centre (usually seen on buses)

IRISH WORDS IN COMMON USE

Gardaí (gardee)	Irish police
Bord Fáilte (board fawlcha)	Irish Tourist Board
Gaeltacht (gwayltockt)	Irish-speaking area
Taoiseach (teeshock)	Irish Prime Minister
Tánaiste (tawnishta)	Irish Deputy Prime Minister
TD (Teachta Dála)	Member of Parliament
Craic (krack)	fun
Céilí (kaylee)	traditional Irish music and dancing

NUMBERS

1	*a haon* (a hayon)	12	*dó dhéag* (doe yayog)
2	*a dó* (a doe)	20	*fiche* (fihah)
3	*a trí* (a tree)	30	*tríocha* (trucha)
4	*a ceathair* (a kahirr)	40	*daichead* (dohhad)
5	*a cúig* (a kooig)	50	*caoga* (kwayga)
6	*a sé* (a shay)	60	*seasca* (shaska)
7	*a seacht* (a shockt)	70	*seachtó* (shockto)
8	*a hocht* (a huckt)	80	*ochtó* (uckto)
9	*a naoi* (a nay)	90	*nócha* (noka)
10	*a deich* (a deh)	100	*céad* (kayd)
11	*a haon déag* (a hayn dayog)	1000	*míle* (meela)

DAYS AND MONTHS

Monday	*Dé Luain* (day loon)
Tuesday	*Dé Máirt* (day mawrt)
Wednesday	*Dé Céadaoin* (day kaydeen)
Thursday	*Déardaoin* (daredeen)
Friday	*Dé hAoine* (day heenya)
Saturday	*Dé Sathairn* (day sahern)
Sunday	*Dé Domhnaigh* (day downig)

HELLOIER THAN THOU

The Irish people are renowned, however erroneously, for being religious and friendly. Who would have thought we could combine the two so well in the simple act of saying 'Hello'? Although, sometimes I'm more inclined to think that the following is an exercise in psyching someone out rather than a profound wish to see them well looked after by saintly types:

Dia dhuit (deea gwit) – Hello
The literal translation here is God be with you, and the tricky thing is, if someone greets you thus, it is not enough to say the same thing back to them; no, you must outdo them in holiness. You have to say:

January	*Eanáir* (annir)
February	*Feabhra* (fyowra)
March	*Márta* (mawrta)
April	*Aibreán* (abbrawn)
May	*Bealtaine* (byowltinna)
June	*Meitheamh* (mehiv)
July	*Iúil* (ool)
August	*Lúnasa* (loonassa)

218

Dia is Muire dhuit (deea smwirra gwit) – Hello (God and Mary be with you)
Of course they may beat you to it and start off the meeting with God and Mary, in which case you say:

Dia is Muire is Pádraig (deea smwirra iss pawdrig) – Hello (God and Mary and St Patrick)
You're really having a rough time of it if someone starts off with that, but there is a response:

Dia is Muire is Pádraig is Bríd (deea smwirra iss pawdrig iss breed) – Hello (God and Mary and St Patrick and St Bridget).
If someone starts off with that, I don't know what to tell you. Make something up!

September	*Meán Fómhair* (manfore)
October	*Deireadh Fómhair* (derrafore)
November	*Mí na Samhna* (mee nah souna)
December	*Mí na Nollag* (mee nah nullog)
day	*lá* (law)
noon	*meánlae* (manlay)
today	*inniu* (innew)

afternoon	*tráthnóna* (trawnona)
yesterday	*inné* (innyay)
night	*oíche* (eeha)
tomorrow	*amárach* (ammawrock)
midnight	*meánoíche* (man eeha)
morning	*maidin* (moddin)

CORK SLANG

In theory we're all speaking the same language but Corkonians have a little mini-dialect all of their own, further complicated by the fact that the exact meaning of a word seems to vary, depending on who you're talking to.

on the batter	on a drinking spree	*lamp*	look
bazzer	haircut	*langer*	an unpleasant person
beoir	girl	*langers*	drunk
fien	guy	*Pana*	Patrick Street
flah	a good-looking person	*have a sconce at*	have a look at
flahed	exhausted	*sham*	a guy that thinks he's cool

13 Further Information

ENTERTAINMENT

Corklife Free bi-monthly magazine with all the latest on Cork fashion and beauty, shopping, nightlife, competitions, etc. Usually available in bars and restaurants.
Totally Cork Free monthly paper with news, reviews and interviews.
WhazOn? Free monthly leaflet listing the latest in arts and entertainment, pubs, restaurants, etc.

MAPS

The Ordnance Survey Discovery series has a range of maps covering the whole county of Cork. They also do the Cork Street Map (detailed map of the city). Otherwise number 87 covers the area around the city, 81 east Cork, 80 and 73 north Cork, 72 and 79 northwest, 85, 86, 88 and 89 west Cork.

BOOKS

Corcoran, Kevin, *West Cork Walks*, O'Brien Press, ISBN-10: 0 86278 928 1
Cotter, Denis, *The Café Paradiso Cookbook*, Atrium, ISBN-10: 0 95353 530 4

Cotter Denis, *Paradiso Seasons*, Atrium, ISBN-10: 0 95353 534 7

Leland, Mary, *The Lie of the Land: Journeys through Literary Cork*, Cork University Press, ISBN-10: 1 85918 231 3

McCarthy, Kieran, *Discover Cork*, O'Brien Press, ISBN-10: 0 86278 817 X

McSweeney, John, *The Golden Age of Cork Cinema*, Rose Arch Publications, ISBN-10: 0 95457 550 4

GAY CORK

The Southern Gay Health Project based in The Other Place (see page 133) is the best place to get information on what's going on. The websites www.gaycork.com and www.gayprojectcork.com are worth checking.

WEBSITES

www.corkkerry.ie Cork tourist office

www.ireland.com/weather and **www.meteireann.ie** Weather.

www.irelandhotels.com Useful when looking for accommodation with specific facilities.

www.irelandconsolidated.com Sells off unsold flight tickets at cheaper prices.

www.ireland.travel.ie Irish Tourist Board.

www.aaroadwatch.ie Useful if planning on driving around Ireland.

www.entertainment.ie Events and reviews.

www.zeitgeist-ireland.com Events.

www.irishroots.net and **www.irishorigins.com** Genealogy resources.

www.irlgov.ie Government website.

www.blueflag.org Safe and clean beaches.

www.cork2005.ie Information on the events that took place during Cork's year as European Capital of Culture.

www.irishnews.com and **www.ireland.com** News coverage.

www.setanta.com Sports coverage.

www.peoplesrepublicofcork.com Crucial website for insight into the wonders of Cork and its inhabitants.

www.corkgigs.com Comprehensive gig guide.

www.heritageisland.com Nationwide visitor attractions.

Index

Page numbers in bold indicate major entries

Abbot's Ale House 122
accommodation **71–85**
    guesthouses 80–2
    hostels 82–4
    hotels 72–80
    self–catering 84–5
air travel 45
airport transfer 67
art galleries **167–71**

banks 53
bars see drinking
Beamish and Crawford Brewery 3,
    157, 162, **178–9**
    Beamish Experience Festival 32
    Beamish Cork Folk Festival 32–3
bed and breakfasts see guesthouses
beer gardens
    Crane Lane Theatre 123, 131, 138
    Franciscan Well Brewery 125–6
    Loafers 128, 133
    Suas 127
    Tom Barry's 128
bike hire 70
Bishop Lucey Park see Peace Park
Blarney **193–5**
    Castle and House 193–4

Blarney continued
    Woollen Mills 194–5
Bonded Warehouses 159
Boole, George 165
bowling
    Mardyke 130
    Leisureplex 190
    Planet Entertainment Centre 191
bus travel
    local 64–5
    international 48
    nationwide 65
    to/from airport 67
business hours 10
Butter Exchange/Shandon Craft
    Centre 165, 171–2
Butter Museum 165, 171–2

cabs see taxis
Cape Clear Island International
    Storytelling Festival 33
car hire 68
car parks see parking
car travel 45–7
cathedrals see churches
children's entertainment **189–91**
    Chuckie's Adventure Play Centre 189

children's entertainment continued
    Cork City Library 189
    Fitzgerald's Park 187–8, 190
    Fota Wildlife Park 190, 200–1
    Leisureplex 190
    Mardyke Arena (UCC) 190–1
    Planet Entertainment Centre 191
    Trabolgan Holiday Village 191
    Chuckie's Adventure Play Centre 189
churches and cathedrals **176–8**
    St Ann's Church/Shandon Bells 165,
        176–7
    St Finbarre's Cathedral 6, 162–3,
        164, 177–8
cinema 135–6
City Hall 159
    Crafts Fair 38
climate XII, 23
Climax at The Liquid Lounge 133
Cobh 6, **195–99**
    history 195
    Mount 197
    Museum 196
    Queenstown Story/Heritage Centre
        198
    Titanic Trail 199
    tourist information centre 196

Cobh *continued*
  Sirius Arts Centre 198
  St Colman's Cathedral 196–7
cocktail bars 114, 129, 127
Collins, Michael 6
consulates *see also* embassies
  local 58–9
  overseas 44
College of Commerce 160
Cork 2005 *see* European Capital of Culture
Cork airport 45
Cork City Gaol and Radio Museum Experience 164, 173–4
Cork Opera House 35, 134–5, 137, 158
  history **179–80**
Cork Public Museum 164, 174–5
Cork School of Music 160
Cork slang *see* language
Cork Vision Centre 180–1
County Hall 164
Crane Lane Theatre 123, 131, 138
Crawford Municipal Art Gallery 158, 167–8
credit/debit cards 53–4
culture and festivals 11 *see also* festivals

Daly Bridge *see* Shaky Bridge
Dickens, Charles 12, 74, 155
drinking **119–30**
drinking hours 120
drisheen *see* tripe and drisheen
driving 45–7

dry cleaning 63
Dúchas *see* Heritage cards

eating and drinking **86–119**
  cafés 108–13
  further afield 117–19
  pubfood 114–15
  restaurants 87–108
  takeaways 115–17
Echo Boys 1, 159
economy 9
electricity 50
Elizabeth Fort 162
embassies *see also* consulates
  local 58–9
  overseas 44
emergency telephone numbers 55–6
English Market *see* Old English Market
entertainment and nightlife **131–8**
European Capital of Culture VII–IX
Everyman Palace Theatre 35, 135

Father Mathew 5, 6, 158
ferries 45–6
festivals **25–37**
  Art Trail 37–8
  Beamish Experience 32
  Beamish Cork Folk 32–3
  Cape Clear Island International Storytelling 33
  City Hall Crafts Fair 38
  Cork Art Fair 32
  Cork Film 34–5
  Cork French Film 28

festivals *continued*
  Cork International Choral 29
  Franciscan Well Easter Beer Fest 30
  Franciscan Well October Beer 36–7
  Frank O'Connor International Short Story 33–4
  Guinness Jazz 35–6
  Heineken Kinsale Rugby Sevens by the Sea 30
  Kinsale Autumn Flavours Festival of Fine Food and Fun 37, 207–8
  Kinsale Fringe Jazz 36
  Mind, Body, Spirit 38–9
  Soundeye Festival of the Arts of the World 31
  Springtime Literature 28
  St Patrick's Day 29
  Woodford Bourne Cork Midsummer 30–1
Firkin Crane 31, 165
Fitzgerald's Park 187–8, 190
Fota 199–201
  House and Gardens 199–200
  Wildlife Park 200–1
Franciscan Well Brewery 125–6, 165
further information **221–3**

GAA *see* Gaelic Athletic Association
Gaelic Athletic Association 18–19
Gaelic football 19
Galí, Beth 8, 158
Gallagher, Rory 16–17, 18, 166
galleries *see* art
Gaol Cross 163–4

225

gay/lesbian **132–4**
genealogy 7
geography 23
getting there and away 45–8
golf 19–21
Gougane Barra Forest Park 201
Granary Theatre 135–6
greyhound racing 21
guesthouses 80–2
guided tours *see* tour operators
Guinness House 160

health 49
    emergency numbers 55–6
    hospitals 59
    pharmacies 59
    travel vaccination centre 60
Heritage cards 192
HiB 123–4
history **2–8**
Holy Trinity Church 156, 161
hostels 82–4
hotels 72–80
    airport 72–3
    city centre 73–7
    eastern outskirts 78–80
    southern outskirts 77–8
hurling 21–2

internet 56
Irish *see* language

Jack Lynch Tunnel 8
Jameson Heritage Centre *see* Midleton

Joyce, James 13, 77, 161

Kennedy, President John F 46, 174
Kinsale **202–8**
    Autumn Flavours Festival of Fine
        Food and Fun 37, 207–8
    Brewing Company 207
    Charles Fort 205–206
    Desmond Castle/Wine Museum
        206–7
    Fringe Jazz Festival 36
    Heineken Rugby Sevens by the Sea
        30
    shops and galleries 205
    restaurants 203–4

lakes 188
language **213–20**
    Cork slang 220
    Irish 214–20
launderette 63
left luggage 63
Leisureplex 190
Lewis Glucksman Gallery 168–9
Library, Cork City 189
literature **12–14**
live music 137–8
Lough, the 188
Luigi Malones 105
Lynch, Jack 8

MacCurtain, Tomas 7, 160
MacSwiney, Terence 7–8, 160
maps 221

Mardyke Arena 190–1
Maryborough House Hotel 77–8
Mathew, Father *see* Father Mathew
media 57–8
medical services *see* health
Melville, Herman 13
Midleton **208–12**
    Barryscourt Castle 208–9
    Old Midleton Distillery 209–11
    Silverstone Dimensions 211
    Stephen Pearce Pottery 211–12
money 50–5
Munster Literature Centre 162, 181–4
museums **171–5**
music 15–18
    live music 137–9

Nagle, Nano 161–2
New Ross 46
newspapers 57
nightclubs 131–33
North Cathedral 166

O'Connor, Frank 13, 182–3
    International Short Story Festival
        33–4
O'Faoláin, Seán 13, 14–15
Old English Market 5, 98, 157, 184–5
opening hours XI
opera 134–5 *see also* Cork Opera
    House
Ó Riada, Seán 15–16

parking 69

parks 187–9
  Fitzgerald's Park 187–8, 190
  Peace Park 157, 188–9
people 9
People's Gallery 169
pharmacies 59
Planet Entertainment Centre 191
population XII
post offices 57
public holidays XII
pubs see drinking
  pub opening hours xi
  pubfood see eating

Queen Victoria 6
Queen's Old Castle 157
Queenstown 6
Queenstown Story 198

radio 58
Radio Museum Experience 173–4
Red Abbey 161
red tape 43
religion 10–11
religious services 60
restaurant opening hours XI
restaurants see eating
road bowling 22–3

self–catering 84–5 see also
  accommodation
Shaky Bridge 164
Shandon
  Bells see St Ann's Church

Shandon continued
  Craft Centre see Butter Exchange
  Steeple see St Ann's Church
shopping 139–52
  antiques 140
  alternative 140–1
  books 142–3
  clothes/fashion 1132–4
  department stores 151–2
  food/wine 145–7
  gifts 147
  home furnishings 148
  jewellery 148
  music 148–9
  outdoor 149–51
  shopping centres 150–2
  supermarkets 150–2
smoking 51, 87, 120
Spenser, Edmund 12–13
Spillane, John 16–17
sport 18–23
St Ann's Church 165, 176–7
St Colman's Cathedral 166, 196–7
St Finbarre 2
  Cathedral 6, 162–3, 164, 177–8
St Patrick's Day 29
synagogue 161

taxis 66–7
telephones 55
  codes XII
television 57–8
Thackeray, William 74, 155
theatres 134–5

theatres continued
  Cork Opera House 134
  Everyman Palace 135
  Granary 135
time XII, 48
tipping X
Titanic Trail 199
Tom Barry's 128
tour operators
  local 60–3
  worldwide 41–3
tourist offices 71
  local 40
  worldwide 41
trains 66
transport 64–70
travellers' cheques 54
tripe and drisheen 13, 98–9, 109, 185
Triskel Arts Centre 138–9, 170–1
Trollope, Anthony 13

UCC see University College Cork
University College Cork 163, 186–7
useful telephone numbers 55–6

vaccinations see health
value added tax 54–5
Vangard Gallery 171
VAT see value added tax

walking tours 153–65
weather see climate
websites 222–3
Women's Gaol see Cork City Gaol

Second edition published April 2007
First published November 2004
Bradt Travel Guides Ltd
23 High Street, Chalfont St Peter, Bucks SL9 9QE, England; www.bradtguides.com
Published in the US by The Globe Pequot Press Inc,
246 Goose Lane, PO Box 480, Guilford, Connecticut 06437-0480
Text copyright © 2007 Linda Fallon   Maps copyright © 2007 Bradt Travel Guides Ltd
Illustrations copyright © Individual photographers and artists
Editorial Project Manager: Emma Thomson

The author and publishers have made every effort to ensure the accuracy of the information in this book
at the time of going to press. However, they cannot accept any responsibility for any loss, injury or
inconvenience resulting from the use of information contained in this guide.

All rights reserved. No part of this publication may be reproduced, stored in a retrieval system, or
transmitted in any form or by any means, electronic, mechanical, photocopying, recording or otherwise
without the prior consent of the publishers.
Requests for permission should be addressed to Bradt Travel Guides Ltd in the UK; or to The Globe
Pequot Press Inc in North and South America.

British Library Cataloguing in Publication Data
A catalogue record for this book is available from the British Library
ISBN-10: 1 84162 196 X   ISBN-13: 978 1 84162 196 8

Photographs LOOK Die Bildagentur der Fotografen GmbH/ Alamy (LBFG/Alamy), Michael Jenner/
Robert Harding (MJ/RH), J Lightfoot/Robert Harding (JL/RH), Julia Bayne/Robert Harding (JB/RH),
Firecrest/Robert Harding (F/RH), Paul Reeves/Robert Harding (PR/RH), Adina Tovy/Robert Harding (AT/RH),
Cork/Kerry Tourism (CK)
Front cover RV parked on Cork Street (LBFG/Alamy) *Title page* Civic monument (MJ/RH), Irish stout (PR/RH)
Maps Steve Munns   **Illustrations** Carole Vincer
Typeset from the author's disc by Wakewing   Printed and bound in Spain by Grafo